Practical English Language Teaching: Listening

MARC HELGESEN
STEVEN BROWN

SERIES EDITOR: DAVID NUNAN

Practical English Language Teaching: Listening

Published by McGraw-Hill ESL/ELT, a business unit of The McGraw-Hill Companies, Inc. 1212 Avenue of the Americas, New York, NY 10020. Copyright © 2007 by The McGraw-Hill Companies, Inc. All rights reserved. No part of this publication may be reproduced or distributed in any form or by any means, or stored in a database or retrieval system, without the prior written consent of The McGraw-Hill Companies, Inc., including, but not limited to, in any network or other electronic storage or transmission, or broadcast for distance learning.

ISBN 13: 978-0-07-328316-6
ISBN 10: 0-07-328316-9
2 3 4 5 6 7 8 9 DOC/DOC 12 11 10 09 08 07 06

ISBN 13: 978-0-07-111921-4 (International Student Book)
ISBN 10: 0-07-111921-3
1 2 3 4 5 6 7 8 9 DOC/DOC 11 10 09 08 07 06

Executive editor: Erik Gundersen
Development editors: Linda O'Roke, Kristin Thalheimer
Production editor: MaryRose Malley
Cover designer: Martini Graphic Services, Inc.
Interior designer: Acento Visual

INTERNATIONAL EDITION ISBN: 0-07-111921-3
Copyright © 2007. Exclusive rights by The McGraw-Hill Companies, Inc., for manufacture and export. This book cannot be re-exported from the country to which it is sold by McGraw-Hill. The International Edition is not available in North America.

The McGraw-Hill Companies

This book is dedicated to our parents
Ken and the memory of Esther Helgesen
Curt and Clara Brown
who, when we were younger, often reminded us: Listen!

Acknowledgements

We would like to thank the following individuals who reviewed the *Practical English Language Teaching* and *Practical English Language Teaching: Listening* manuscripts at various stages of their development, and whose commentary was instrumental in helping us shape these professional reference volumes:

Kathleen M. Bailey, Monterey Institute of International Studies, Monterey, California, USA

Ronald Carter, Centre for English Language Education, Department of English Studies, University of Nottingham, UK

Andy Curtis, The English School, Kingston, Ontario, Canada

Nicholas Dimmitt, Asian Institute of Technology, Pathumthani, Thailand

Fernando Fleurquin, ALIANZA, Montevideo, Uruguay

Donald Freeman, School for International Training, Brattleboro, Vermont, USA

Donald Occhuizzo, World Learning/School for Internacional Training; formerly Alumni, Sao Paulo, Brazil

Betsy Parrish, Hamline University, St. Paul, Minnesota, USA

Michael Rost, Author/Researcher, San Francisco, California, USA

Kathy Z. Weed

We would like to thank Mike Rost, both for his feedback on the manuscript and also for all we have learned from him over the years. Also, thanks to the experts who provided "Top five" lists for Chapter 5: John Flowerdew, Tony Lynch, Lindsay Miller, David Nunan, Jack Richards, and Mike Rost. Thanks to colleagues Hiroshi Adachi, Gerry Lassche, Helen Kim Lassche, Michelle Milner, Chaz Pugliese, Dorolyn Smith, and especially, Brenda Hayashi (who must have heard, "Sorry to bother you, but can I run something by you?" a thousand times). Thanks to John Fanselow and Terry Royce for inviting us to teach at Columbia University Teachers College M.A. TESOL Program, Tokyo, and to our students there who piloted much of the material in this book. Thanks to Ellen Shaw, with whom we began *Active Listening,* and Deborah Goldblatt, who gave us insight into the project over the years. Finally, a special thank you to the *Practical English Language Teaching* team: David Nunan, who invited us to be part of the series, our wonderful editors Linda O'Roke, Erik Gundersen, and Kristin Thalheimer, and Hajime Shishido, Japanese ELT sales manager, who has an excellent understanding for what the market really needs.

Table of Contents

Foreword

Vision and purpose

The *Practical English Language Teaching* series is designed for practicing teachers or teachers in preparation who may or may not have formal training in second and foreign language teaching methodology. The core volume in this series, *Practical English Language Teaching*, provides an overall introduction to key aspects of language teaching methodology in an accessible yet not trivial way. The purpose of this book is to explore the teaching of listening in greater depth than was possible in the core volume, while at the same time remaining both comprehensive and accessible.

Features

- A clear orientation to the teaching of listening including important definitions, an introduction to the processes behind listening, and a look at the overall approach to teaching listening in the classroom.

- A detailed treatment of teaching listening at beginner, intermediate, and advanced levels, providing practical techniques for teaching and assessing listening at each of these levels.

- Reflection questions inviting readers to think about critical issues in language teaching and Action tasks requiring readers to apply the ideas, principles, and techniques to the teaching of listening in their own situation.

- A CD containing the audio segments that accompany many of the textbook examples included in the book.

- A great deal of practical illustration from a wide range of textbooks as well as discussion of how to apply the textbooks in the classroom.

- A "key issues" chapter that looks at listening beyond the classroom and provides suggestions for dealing with the use of technology and catering to different learning styles and strategies. This chapter also features tips from leading researchers and teachers of listening.

- Suggestions for books, articles, and websites offering resources for additional up-to-date information.

- An expansive glossary offering short and straightforward definitions of core language teaching terms.

Audience

As with the overview volume, this book is designed for both experienced and novice teachers. It should also be of value to those who are about to join the profession. It will update the experienced teacher on current theoretical and practical approaches to teaching listening. The novice teacher will find step-by-step guidance on the practice of language teaching.

Overview

Chapter 1

The first chapter provides an orientation to listening in a second or foreign language. The chapter also introduces key principles for teaching and assessing listening.

Chapters 2–4

Chapters 2–4 introduce you to the teaching of listening to beginner, intermediate, and advanced students respectively. Each chapter follows the format below.

Chapter 5

The final chapter explores key issues including the teaching of listening in working with learners who have different learning styles and strategies, using technology, and giving learners ways to practice outside the classroom. It also features tips on teaching listening by leading experts.

Chapter structure for Chapters 2–4

Goals: Summarizes what you should know and be able to do after having read the chapter and completed the Reflection and Action tasks.

Introduction: Gives an overview of the chapter.

Syllabus design issues: Outlines the approaches to listening that are relevant at different levels.

Principles for teaching listening: Introduces, discusses, and illustrates appropriate principles for teaching listening at different levels.

Tasks and materials: Describes and illustrates techniques and exercises for teaching listening at each level.

Listening in the classroom: Introduces issues such as lesson planning that affect what we do in the classroom.

CD audio examples: Accompanies many of the examples included in the book. We encourage you to actually listen to the audio CD as you read the example. As you do, notice both what you are listening to and what students just learning the language would likely do and think about to make sense of what they are hearing.

Techniques for assessment: Introduces practical techniques for assessing learners in the classroom.

Conclusion: Reviews the goals of the chapter and how they were discussed within the chapter.

Further reading: Lists articles or books to enhance your knowledge of teaching listening.

Helpful Web sites: Provides ideas for Web resources for teaching listening.

A personal note from the authors

Becoming and developing as a teacher is a rather personal, experiential process—one that is different for everyone. To facilitate that, we have tried to write this book in a friendly, accessible style. We envision it as a conversation between colleagues. And, because we believe that one learns best by observing and by doing, we have tried to use a lot of examples. In this way we are trying, on the pages of a book, to replicate what goes on in our classrooms. We hope you find it useful.

Chapter **One**

What is listening?

At the end of the chapter, you should be able to:

Goals

 state your own definition of listening.

 explain the term *active listening.*

 understand the terms *top-down* and *bottom-up processing.*

 identify the stages of a listening lesson.

 identify types of listening.

✔ **understand** principles of assessment.

1. Introduction

The aim of this book is to help you effectively teach listening to students of **English as a Second Language** or **English as a Foreign Language (ESL or EFL)**. We hope to share with you practical information about how ESL and EFL listening works and how you can teach it effectively. In a sense, we'd like to invite you into our own classrooms to see how our students learn, and share the ideas behind what we are doing as teachers. To lay the foundation for that, this chapter will introduce a few key concepts about listening and how to teach it. We will look at several definitions of listening. Next, we will consider approaches to listening, stressing that, although listening is a **receptive skill**, it is also a very active one. We will then consider **direction of processing**—how people try to make sense of what they hear. This is followed by a section on teaching listening which stresses tasks and the types of listening learners need experience with. Finally, we will consider ways to assess learners' listening abilities and progress.

Reflection

What have you listened to today? Write at least nine things. List different types of things you've listened to.

- _____
- _____
- _____
- _____
- _____
- _____
- _____
- _____
- _____

Of course, every day you listen to a variety of different things. How you listen and what you do when you listen depends on your purpose. Throughout this chapter, we'll come back to the list of things you have actually listened to today.

2.   What is listening?

Because it is something we do every day, listening seems simple. Yet, when one is listening in a second or foreign language, we can see more easily how complex listening really is. Let's start by looking at some definitions of listening.

- "Listening is an active, purposeful processing of making sense of what we hear" (Helgesen, 2003, p. 24).
- (Listening is the) "mental process of constructing meaning from spoken input" (Rost, 2002, p. 279).
- "Listening comprehension (is) the process of understanding speech in a first or second language. The study of listening comprehension in second language learning focuses on the role of individual linguistic units (e.g., **phonemes**, words, grammatical structures) as well as the role of the listener's expectations, the situation and context, background knowledge and topic" (Richards and Schmidt, 2002, p. 313).
- "[L]istening is conceived of as an active process in which listeners select and interpret information which comes from auditory and visual clues in order to define what is going on and what the speakers are trying to express" (Rubin, 1995, p. 7).

Reflection

1. Look at the definitions of listening above. Which characteristics seem to be in more than one definition?

2. If you had written a definition for listening before you read the definitions above, which characteristics would you have included? How would you revise that definition now?

Notice that the definitions for listening all use words like *active* and *construct*. It is clear that the listener is doing more than simply decoding what is heard. Rubin completes her definition by saying that *active* means listeners get information (from visual and auditory clues) and relate this information to what they already know. *Select* means that in the process of making sense of the **input**, listeners use only part of the incoming information. *Interpret* means that in trying to make sense of the input, listeners use their background knowledge as well as the new information to decipher what is going on and to figure out what speakers intend.

3. Approaches to listening

We listen to many things every day. We hear even more. What's the difference? In this section, we'll start by considering the differences between listening and hearing, an essential concept in teaching listening.

Action

1. Think about the following sentences. What do *listen* and *hear* mean in each?
   a. Listen to me.

   b. I like talking to her because she's a great listener.

   c. A: What was that noise?
      B: I didn't hear anything.

   d. A: I'm tired. Let's take a break.
      B: I hear you.

   e. I need to go upstairs for a minute. Could you listen for the doorbell?

   f. Radio station testimonial/advertisement: "I hear you guys everywhere, even when I don't listen."

2. How are *listening* and *hearing* different, both in these sentences and your own understanding of the words? Write your answers below.

   Characteristics of *listening:* _____

   _____

   Characteristics of *hearing:* _____

   _____

Listening vs. hearing

Most people's answers to the Action box above will include the fact that a listener is an active partner in the listening process. When your alarm clock goes off in the morning, you hear it whether you want to or not. If it's a special day–one where you wake up before your alarm–you may lie in bed, listening for it. Then you get up. Or say you are cooking in the kitchen and the TV is on in the background. Are you listening to it or just hearing it? It depends on how much attention you are paying to it. You may just hear it, but when something important comes on–the weather or news, perhaps–you actually listen. The point is that listening is a very active skill. It requires the active attention–and an active intention–on the part of the hearer.

This recognition of listening as an **active skill** is relatively new. For years, people thought of listening and reading as **passive skills** while speaking and writing were active skills. Indeed, until the late 1970s, not much attention was paid to ESL and EFL listening at all. Prior to that, if it was thought about at all, listeners were thought of as *human tape recorders:* They took in a bit of information, held it in a sort of medium-term memory, and used it. We now recognize that listening is much more complex than that. Listeners are actively paying attention and working on understanding and interpreting what they hear.

Instead of thinking of listening as passive, it is useful to understand it, along with reading, as a receptive skill. This is in contrast with speaking and writing, which are **productive skills**. It is an important distinction. As we'll see, we can often understand language we couldn't possibly produce. This will have major implications when we look at teaching listening and the nature of listening tasks. For now, however, it is enough just to note the difference in receptive and productive levels. If you've ever studied a foreign language or traveled abroad, you've probably experienced being able to understand things that you can't actually say. Or, if you've watched a film in a variety of English that you don't speak or haven't studied, you've heard and understood a dialect even though you would find it difficult to say exactly what you heard, using the exact words and expressions. What you are noticing is the difference between receptive and productive language.

Reflection

Go back to the items you listed in the Reflection box on page 2.

1. Which of the items were *listening?* Which were *hearing?*

2. If all the things you listed were *listening,* can you add other things that you heard but didn't have to listen to or for?

3. What, if anything, did you do in response to each item you listed? Which required a productive response from you? Which only required reception (understanding)?

Another way to think about listening is the distinction between **reciprocal listening** and **non-reciprocal listening**. Reciprocal listening is between people. When we have conversations, we listen to each other, add our ideas, and give feedback (like the **back channel** phrases *Uh huh* and *Really?*). Non-reciprocal listening is the kind of listening we're familiar with from language classes. The teacher plays an audio recording and students do a task, or the teacher dictates and students write. A lot of listening in language textbooks is really eavesdropping ("CIA English") where students are overhearing a conversation between other people. Lectures fall somewhere between reciprocal and non-reciprocal listening, though most of the time they are non-reciprocal. Some very active lecturers may have an interactive style and students may be encouraged, or required, to respond with their own ideas, or answer questions.

4. Listening in action

Top-down vs. bottom-up processing

Anything we hear, of course, can be **input**. To go back to our hearing/listening distinction, there's a lot we hear but do not pay attention (listen) to. When we do pay attention, we begin to process the input. To understand listening, we have to consider how people process this input. A useful way of looking at this is by considering **bottom-up** and **top-down processing** (Rumelhart, 1977; Flowerdew and Miller, 2005).

Bottom-up processing is trying to make sense of what we hear by focusing on the different parts: the vocabulary, the grammar or **functional phrases**, sounds, etc. Top-down processing, on the other hand, starts with background knowledge called **schema**. This can be content schema (general knowledge based on life experience and previous learning) or textual schema (knowledge of language and content used in a particular situation: the language you need at a bank is different than what you need when socializing with friends).

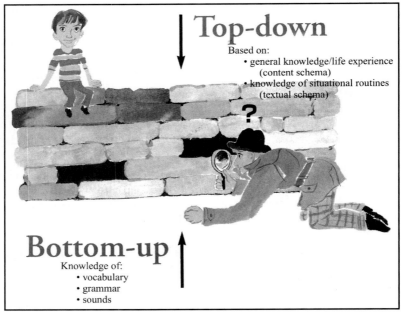

Figure 1: Bottom-up and top-down processing

To understand this more easily, consider the metaphor in Figure 1. Imagine a brick wall. If you are at the bottom of the wall, looking at it brick-by-brick like the detective in the picture, it is easy to see all the parts.

However, it is difficult to get a good, overall view of the wall. And when you get to a missing brick (to take the metaphor a step further—an unknown word or a new piece of grammar), there is nothing to focus on.

If, on the other hand, you are sitting on the top of the wall, you are looking in a different direction. You have a good view of the landscape. You see what is going on. Of course, you miss a lot of details because of the distance, but you generally understand the scene. You don't even notice the bricks in the wall that are supporting you, and your view is very different than that of the person looking at the parts.

It is not surprising that many learners tend to listen to a foreign language "bottom-up." In school, we often teach based on the "building blocks" of word and structures. Students, who have a less than complete knowledge of the new language, grab for the pieces they understand. Unfortunately, the results can be frustrating.

Action

Read the passage below. Then write a title for it.

Title: _____

Sally first tried setting loose a team of gophers. The plan backfired when a dog chased them away.

She then entertained a group of teenagers and was delighted when they brought their motorcycles.

Unfortunately, she failed to find a Peeping Tom listed in the Yellow Pages.

The crabgrass might have worked, but she didn't have a fan that was sufficiently powerful.

The obscene phone calls gave her hope until the number was changed.

She thought about calling a door-to-door salesman but decided to hang up a clothesline instead.

It was the installation of blinking neon lights across the street that did the trick. She eventually framed the ad from the classified section.

(Stein and Albridge, 1978, cited in Richards, 1990, p. 52)

As you were reading, you likely had a series of unrelated pictures flash through your mind: gophers, motorcyclists, a clothesline, a phone book, etc. But you probably had difficulty coming up with a title because you didn't know—and couldn't figure out—the context. You were reading bottom-up, trying to understand the whole by only looking at the parts. You probably felt the frustration of this one-way type of processing–it was like looking at bricks but not seeing the landscape. If you had known the topic–*Getting rid of a troublesome neighbor*–it would have made sense. As you read that topic a moment ago, everything probably started to make sense. You could imagine that all these things were actions that could be taken to get someone to move away. Students who are putting too much reliance on figuring out all the pieces of what they hear are likely to experience the same frustration that you felt reading the "Sally" passage. You likely understood all the words. When learners don't understand, they often figure it is a vocabulary problem. No doubt vocabulary is essential to learning language, but it is not the only issue. With listening, the way they are thinking about what they hear is important.

While over-reliance on "bottom-up" processing can get listeners into trouble, so can the opposite.

Action

Read the passage below. As you do, ask yourself:

• What do I imagine the scene is like?
• What do I think will happen next?

When I first came to Japan, I met a British teacher working at the same school as I. He told me about his first summer in Japan. Japan is really hot. Very hot and humid. One day, he was sitting at home.

• What is the scene like?
• What will happen next?

So, he's sitting at home and he hears a song coming mechanically from the speakers of a truck. The song was "Camptown Races." It was kind of like it was played with bells.

"Great," my friend said.

• What is the scene like?
• What will happen next?

"Great," my friend said. "An ice cream truck."

He walked out on the street and sure enough, there was a truck: A garbage truck. He didn't know that in parts of Japan, garbage trucks play a melody to let people know that they had come, and people could come out and pick up their garbage cans.

As you read, did you make the same assumption as the teacher? If you come from a culture where music from a truck signals ice cream, you might easily have made the same misinterpretation. Or, if mechanical music from the street indicates something else in your culture, you might have made a different assumption. Whatever assumption you made, you based it on your own schema—your knowledge and expectations of a particular situation.

As you can see, putting too much focus on either bottom-up or top-down processing leads to misunderstanding. One of your jobs as a listening teacher is to help your students learn to balance the two kinds of processing.

Reflection

1. Read this true story that happened to me a few years ago. As you do, notice how top-down and bottom-up information mix to help the listener understand what is being asked.

Visiting Rome, I was in the courtyard in front of St. Peter's Basilica. A woman came up and asked me something in Italian, a language I don't know. I looked at her with a puzzled expression. She asked a question again, this time simplifying it to one word, "Cappella?" I didn't know what she meant but repeated, "Cappella?" She asked again, "Cappella Sistina?" Then I understood that she wanted to know if the big church in front of us was the "Sistine Chapel." I replied, "No, San Pietro." (I did know the Italian name of St. Peter's.) I pointed to a building on the right side of the courtyard and said "Sistine." She smiled, said "grazie," and walked off toward the Sistine Chapel.

2. When was I using top-down processing? When was it bottom-up?

3. Have you experienced trying to communicate in another language? What problems did you have? Can you think of ways in which top-down or bottom-up information helped you understand?

What happened in the short interaction described in the Reflection box was a combination of bottom-up and top-down processing. Recognizing the single word "Sistine" told me that "cappella" must mean "chapel." We were standing in front of buildings. She was asking a question about places. My top-down knowledge of what people might talk about—especially to strangers—said that she must be asking for directions. With a friend, you might comment on the size of the buildings or their beauty or something else, but with a stranger, asking for directions or asking someone to take a picture seem the only likely topics. Using both bottom-up data (the word "Sistine") and the top-down data (likely language function), I was able to understand what she wanted.

5. Teaching listening

A listening lesson often has three parts: pre-listening, listening task, and post-listening (optional). In this section, we will examine each part and the reasons they are important.

Pre-listening

A teacher rarely walks into class, puts a CD or DVD in the machine, says "Listen," and hits the start button. Just as you need to stretch your muscles and warm up before exercising, your students need to warm-up their non-native language skills before doing an exercise. A "pre-listening" warm-up task is more than just an introduction to the topic, although that aspect of it is important. Pre-listening is how we can help learners achieve the balance between top-down and bottom-up processing. In many warm-up activities, learners do tasks to "activate their schemata" (the plural form of schema)— essentially reminding themselves of content related to what they will hear as well as vocabulary and, at times, forms that will carry the content. When learners use both top-down and bottom-up processing, this is called **interactive processing** (Peterson, 2001).

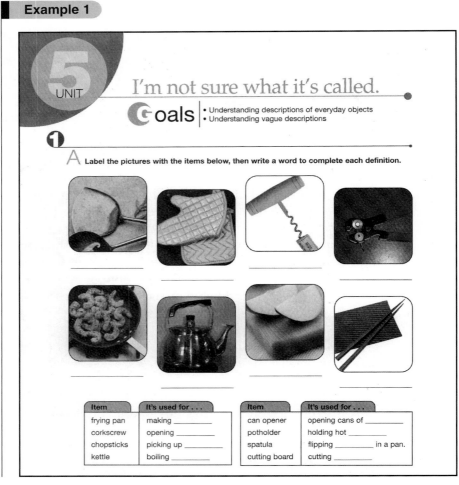

Example 1

UNIT **5**

I'm not sure what it's called.

Goals : • Understanding descriptions of everyday objects
• Understanding vague descriptions

1

A. Label the pictures with the items below, then write a word to complete each definition.

Item	It's used for . . .	Item	It's used for . . .
frying pan	making _____	can opener	opening cans of _____
corkscrew	opening _____	potholder	holding hot _____
chopsticks	picking up _____	spatula	flipping _____ in a pan.
kettle	boiling _____	cutting board	cutting _____

Listen In, Book 3 (Nunan, 2003, p. 28)

Example 1 shows two kinds of schema activation. In the main listening task, students will hear conversations about objects and their uses. They probably don't know the English names for some of the objects. They probably will be able to focus on the uses of the items to understand what is being talked about. In Example 1, students see pictures of eight items. The vocabulary is provided but not defined at the bottom of the page. Students must match the picture and the label. So, now they have the names for the items (word level, bottom-up knowledge). Then students have to finish the definitions with their own examples. These examples, of course, come from their own experience and world knowledge (content and concept level, top-down knowledge). In the process, they generate vocabulary and the grammatical forms that will later carry the information for the main listening task. Notice how clues are embedded. "Spatula" may be an unknown word. The clue "flipping ___ in a pan" can focus the learners' attention on the spatula. If they look at the other pictures, they will notice that most of the items are not used for flipping things.

Listening tasks

Traditional listening materials often had learners listen to a **text**—in teaching listening, any listening passage is referred to as a text. After they listen, the learners answer some comprehension questions. There are a number of problems with this approach. First of all, in real life, we almost always know why we are listening to something. When the comprehension questions follow a listening text, the learner may not know what to listen for. Also, when questions are answered after listening to the text, and learners get the answers wrong, you don't know if it was because they didn't understand, they understood but forgot, they were focusing on something else so understood the wrong part of the text, or if there was some other problem.

Using tasks when teaching listening gets you away from these problems. Tasks imply that one is listening for a purpose. Sometimes we want to catch very specific information. At other times, we are listening in a more general, global way. Still other times, we have to make inferences. That is, we are listening for meaning that is given or implied, but not stated directly.

Look at Example 2 on page 12. As you can see, the text (found on the audio CD or in Appendix 2 on page 162) can be used for several different listening tasks. In Task 1, the learners are listening for the main idea. Although both the doctor and the school are mentioned, the main point of the conversation is school. This type of listening task is called **global listening** or **listening for gist**.

Example 2

CD Track 2

Try it again. Two friends are talking on the telephone.
Each time you listen, think about the information you need.

1 **Listening for the main idea**
Listen. What is the most important idea?
Check (✔) your answer.

☐ going to the doctor   ☐ school

2 **Listening for specific information**
Listen. Which page numbers should she read?
Write the page numbers.

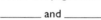 and _____

3 **Listening "between the lines"**
Listen again. Did both students go to school today?
Check (✔) your answer.

☐ Yes   ☐ No

You heard the same conversation three times.
Each time, you listened for different reasons.
Always think about why you are listening.

Active Listening 1 (Helgesen and Brown, 1995, p. 5)

In Task 2, the learners need to remember the pages that are the homework. The learners are **listening for specific information**.

In Task 3, the learners are **making inferences**–listening between the lines. They never actually hear that Joan was not at school today, but it can be understood from the situation.

Of course, just having the learners aware of the task before they listen improves comprehension and success–they are aware of their task, so are less likely to engage in random listening.

Action

1. Go back to the Reflection box on page 2.

2. Look at the things you listened to.
   When were you listening for specific information? Write "S" next to the line.
   When were you listening for gist/general understanding? Write "G".
   Were there cases where you had to infer meaning? Write "I".
   Were there other purposes? How would you identify your purposes? Write a description (examples: enjoyment, entertainment).

   Share your answers with a classmate or colleague.

Of course, when we listen, we are usually combining different types of listening. Your global understanding of a situation may help you pick out specific bits of information. Catching specific details may help you follow the gist. **Inferencing** usually happens when you are listening for some other purpose and the content doesn't state the information explicitly.

To demonstrate how critical the nature of the listening task is in being able to catch necessary information, try this. You will listen to a short text in Korean. Even if you don't understand Korean, you will be able to do the task.

Seoul is now served by Incheon International Airport, one of the most modern in the world. Before this new airport opened, people used Gimpo Airport. Gimpo had three terminals, two international and one domestic. A shuttle bus traveled among the three. Imagine you are on that shuttle bus. You need to find out which terminal the airline you want is in.

You will hear the announcement on the shuttle bus. Before you listen, decide which airline you are looking for.

Check (✓) your choice

☐ Asiana   ☐ China

☐ Garuda Indonesia   ☐ Japan Airlines

☐ Singapore   ☐ Swiss

Audio

CD Tracks 3 and 4

Now listen to CD Track 3. The bus is approaching a terminal. Will you get off at this stop? Check your answer.

☐ Yes   ☐ No

Now listen to CD Track 4 (English) to check your answer.

Unless you understand Korean, you were experiencing this the way a person who is a complete beginner has to try to listen for specific information. You anticipated the information you needed by choosing the airline. Then you listened, not to understand everything and use what you needed, but rather to pick out the keywords you needed—Asiana, Garuda, Indonesia, or Swiss. Going back to our brick wall metaphor, it was as if you ignored most of the bricks and only picked out a few necessary ones.

Notice that the specificity of the task allowed you to do it as you listened. If you had a task that required more production—for example, to write down the names of the airlines you understood—it would have been much more difficult.

Example 3

CD Track 5

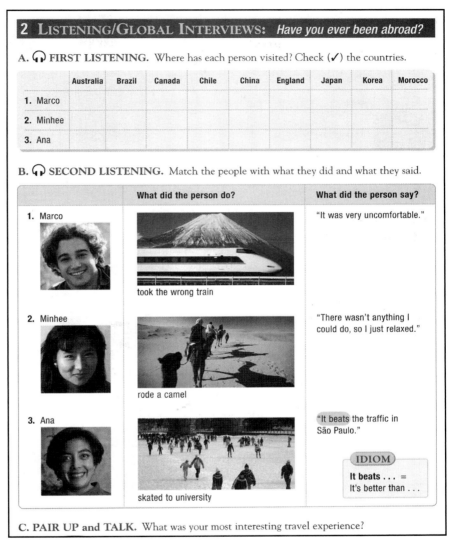

2 LISTENING/GLOBAL INTERVIEWS: *Have you ever been abroad?*

A. 🎧 **FIRST LISTENING.** Where has each person visited? Check (✓) the countries.

	Australia	Brazil	Canada	Chile	China	England	Japan	Korea	Morocco
1. Marco									
2. Minhee									
3. Ana									

B. 🎧 **SECOND LISTENING.** Match the people with what they did and what they said.

	What did the person do?	What did the person say?
1. Marco	took the wrong train	"It was very uncomfortable."
2. Minhee	rode a camel	"There wasn't anything I could do, so I just relaxed."
3. Ana	skated to university	"It beats the traffic in São Paulo."

> **IDIOM**
>
> It beats . . . =
> It's better than . . .

C. PAIR UP and TALK. What was your most interesting travel experience?

ICON 1 (Freeman, Graves, and Lee, 2005, p. 63)

Generally, listening tasks are completed as the students listen. Look at and listen to the audio for Example 3. Notice that the tasks are quite simple. The first time the learners listen, they simply check the countries the students on the audio program have visited. Then they listen again. This time they match speakers, activities, and comments. Note that the learners never have to spend a lot of time writing long answers. Longer answers have a place at higher levels, but it is important for learners to be able to focus on their listening skills. Also, since we know listening is receptive, the learners' responses should not involve a lot of production.

Example 4

CD Track 6

Good News, Bad News (Barnard, 1998, p. 29)

Before we discuss Example 4, listen to the audio and do the exercises. Example 4 shows two different types of tasks, both of which are in the general category of global listening. First, students hear a short news story. They identify the correct summary. Then they look at six pictures. Before they listen again, they number the pictures to show the sequence of the story. Then they listen again to confirm their guesses. In the process of guessing before they listen, they have to really look at all six pictures and notice what is happening in each. This allows them to activate their schemata. Some teachers take this a step further by having students do the task in pairs. Students say what they think is happening in each picture. This encourages the activation of vocabulary for the ideas/actions shown in the pictures. Also, since they have made a guess as to what they think happened, most learners are more motivated to really pay attention when they listen again to see if they are right.

Note that the learners hear the same recording twice. In her classic book on teaching listening, *Teaching Listening Comprehension* (1984), Penny Ur points out what she calls "the apparent need of the foreign-language learner to perceive and comprehend everything he hears, even though he would not do so in his native language." She goes on to suggest that the "learner who tries to understand every single word…will be handicapped both by his failure to do so…and his success" (p. 14). This means if learners don't catch everything, they are frustrated and if they do, they are listening in a way that doesn't help since they don't "ignore or *skim* unimportant items" (p. 15).

Giving learners an additional task allows them to hear something a second time, therefore understanding more of it, but they are listening for a different purpose. Nunan (1999) calls this "progressively structured" listening instruction. It helps to deal with the need Ur mentions while increasing task awareness.

The listening task in Example 3 (page 15) is followed by a cloze (fill-in-the-blanks) activity. This task gives learners a chance to work with listening for specific information. It also makes sure they have had practice with both top-down and bottom-up listening.

Post-listening

The range of post-listening activities is at least as wide as listening tasks themselves. At times, post-listening may be as simple as checking the answers to comprehension questions, either by the teacher telling the learners what the correct answers are, by eliciting answers from the students themselves, or by having students compare their answers in pairs or small groups.

Sometimes, that's all teachers have time for, or all that the curriculum requires. It is useful to note that, although listening is a separate skill, most skills are not and should not be taught entirely separately. Speaking activities where learners talk to each other require listening as well and, very often, post-listening activities are speaking tasks. Look at Example 3 again (p. 15).

The final step, "Pair up and Talk," allows learners to personalize the activity. They talk about their own experiences, using the listening text as a model.

After Example 4 (page 16), students do a pair work activity thematically tied to a prison escape (not shown). They draw an escape plan on a map and describe it to a partner who tries to follow the directions.

These kinds of activities not only help students learn by asking them to use and re-use the language they've heard, but they are motivating. They make the language real.

6. Assessing listening

Assessment is important both because as teachers we need to give grades and because we want to provide feedback (Brindley, 2003). Assessment is quite complex and means many things to many people. For example, every time learners do a task and successfully complete it, they are getting some feedback on their own. That's a form of **self-assessment**. We can also provide specific tasks that help learners assess their own learning, and we will discuss some of those later in this book. We can also assess learners through non-traditional means. In this section, we're going to look at formal assessment, because it's both very important and often misunderstood. Formal classroom assessment–tests–should be similar to other things the learners have been doing in class. A basic principle of assessment is that it is only fair and useful to test what has been taught, so testing will often not be so different than the rest of a course.

Bailey (2005) identifies four key concepts in testing: **validity**, **reliability**, **practicality**, and **washback**.

Validity means that we are actually measuring what we are trying to measure. If, for example, we are doing a listening test that requires writing long answers, we may be testing writing rather than listening. If we test in a computer lab and some learners don't know how to use computers, we could be testing their technical ability rather than their listening. Tests should test what has actually been taught.

Reliability means that test results are consistent. A person being evaluated at different times or by different people would get a similar score. If, for example, you are doing an interview test and, after a long day, tend to give lower or higher scores, that test is not reliable.

Practicality means that the demands of giving the test are reasonable. If you are interested in CALL (Computer Assisted Language Learning) but end up teaching in an undeveloped country without technology, computer-based tests wouldn't be practical. If you are in a secondary school or university and have hundreds of students–not at all unusual in some countries–an interview test would probably not be practical.

Washback is the effect that the test has on what is taught and how it is taught. This can happen either by course content being included or excluded. If we emphasize listening in a course but only give a "paper and pencil" test that doesn't involve listening, we devalue listening as an important part of the course. As Rost (2002, p. 173) points out, "If teaching is not consistent with testing, or if instruction provided doesn't help them with test performance, students are dissatisfied. As a result, teachers begin 'teaching for the test' (even if they believe the test itself is invalid)."

Reflection

1. What is your experience with taking tests in foreign or second language classes? What different types of tests were used? Did they reflect what you had studied?

2. How did you prepare for the tests?

3. If you have visited a culture where a language you have studied is used, did the testing reflect the kind of language you would actually need to use?

Testing techniques

Throughout this book we'll consider different testing techniques. As a preview, consider this list from Rost (2002). It outlines the major types of tests.

1. **Discrete-item tests**
   - Multiple-choice questions following a listening text (responses scored right or wrong)
   - Open questions following presentation of a listening text (questions scored on a scale of correctness and completeness)
   - Standardized test scores (e.g., TOEFL® or TOEIC®)
2. **Integrative tests**
   - Open summarizing of a listening text (scored on scales of accuracy and inclusion of facts and ideas)
   - Cloze summarizing of a text (scored on correct completions of blanks)
   - Dictation, complete or partial (score based on supplying the correct missing words)
3. **Communicative tests**
   - Written communicative tasks involving listening (scored on the basis of successful completion of a task, such as writing a complaint letter after hearing a description of a problem)

4. Interview tests
- Face-to-face performances with the teacher or another student (scored based on a checklist of items, such as appropriate response to questions, appropriate use of clarification questions)
- Extended oral interview (scoring is keyed to a scale of native-like behaviors, such as the Foreign Service Institute scale)

5. Self-assessment
- Learner rates self on given criteria, via questionnaire
- Learner provides holistic assessment of own abilities via oral or written journal entries

6. Portfolio assessment
- Learner is observed and evaluated periodically throughout the course on behavior in tasks and other class activities: observations may be audio or videotaped
- Portfolio may include any or all of the above types of objective and subjective measures

One very important distinction in testing is the difference between **normative testing** and **criterion-referenced testing**. Norm-referenced tests (Figure 2) compare students to each other. Criterion-referenced tests (Figure 3, page 21) compare students to what they should have learned/achieved.

Some teachers mistakenly believe that grades for a course should form a bell curve: Most students, these teachers say, are average, so perhaps half ought to get Cs. Another 15% should be on each side of the peak, so they get Bs and Ds respectively. And only about 10% should get the top level As (and of course, their 10% counterparts at the other end of the spectrum fail).

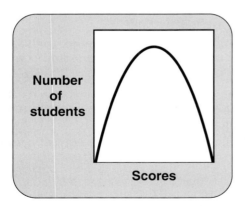

Figure 2: Norm-referenced tests

Wrong concept, wrong test

A bell curve is how you grade a norm-referenced test. A norm-referenced test compares students to each other. That is fine for an IQ test or something like the TOEIC® or TOEFL®. The important thing to understand is that normed tests do not measure the students against what they know. They measure them against each other.

Remember the key concept in educational testing: *It is only fair to test students on what you have taught them.*

Given that, you should not be "grading on a curve." You should be giving criterion-referenced tests. That means you figure out what you are teaching (the criteria for passing the class). Test the learners on that. And, assuming you've been doing a good job, most students should do well.

This means you ought to have a scale that looks more like this: A few are at the low end, but most learners will have done well. If they learned what they were supposed to, they should get a good grade.

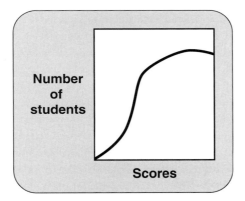

Figure 3: Criterion-referenced tests

Some people ask, "Isn't that 'dumbing things down?' Not everyone does as well as each other." Again, it has to do with what you are testing. If you ask them to learn x, and they do, they should pass, even if someone else learned $x+1$ (or $x+2$ or $x+10$).

Think about it this way: Let's say you are going to take your driver's license test. You've gone to driving school. You've studied the manual. You've practiced. You are ready to take the test. You get to the driving center that day and notice that the person standing in line next to you is Formula 1 driver Michael Schumacher. He's arguably the best race car driver in the world. A better driver than you, no doubt. Does that mean your grade on the test—whether you pass or not—should somehow be impacted by the fact that he is taking the test? Of course not. You were asked to learn x (how to drive, rules of the road, etc.). The fact that Schumacher learned $x+1$ has nothing to do with your skill. You met the criterion.

And, in class, if most of your students do well, that's great. As we've said elsewhere, "They have reached the 'criterion,' the highest level. They learned what you taught. That's not just OK. That's success!" (Helgesen & Brown, 2001)

7. Conclusion

In this chapter, we have attempted to lay the foundation for understanding the basics of teaching listening to students of a second or foreign language. Listening, although a receptive skill, is a very active process. We introduced the ideas of directions of processing, making the case that both top-down and bottom-up are necessary and useful. We suggested that most listening lessons include pre-listening, which activates learners' previous knowledge (schema), listening tasks, and post-listening exercises which often include speaking activities. We considered a range of assessment options. In the next three chapters, we'll look specifically at helping students at different levels improve their listening skills.

The great French director Jean-Luc Godard once said, "all films should have a beginning, middle, and end, but not necessarily in that order." Sometimes books are the same way. Of course, we wrote this one assuming that people would read from front to back, but we know people read books in different ways, depending on their needs and interests.

We end the book with a series of "Top five ideas for teaching listening" lists by various experts. The lists summarize many of the ideas we wrote about in the book. You might want to consider reading those lists now. They start on page 146. Of course, many of the ideas will be new, so you won't completely understand the "how" and "why" of them just yet. But they will preview the ideas and perhaps whet your curiosity. Then when you get the lists later, after you've read the whole book, they will make even more sense.

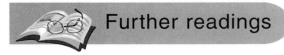

Further readings

Flowerdew, J. and L. Miller. 2005. *Second Language Listening: Theory and Practice.*

A useful and very readable guide to the subject.

Mendelsohn, D. and J. Rubin (eds.). 1995. *A Guide for the Teaching of Second Language Listening.*

An excellent introduction. Gary Buck's chapter, "How to become a good listening teacher," is particularly recommended.

Helpful Web sites

Speech, Pronunciation, & Listening Interest Section (www.soundsofenglish.org)

This is the site of the Speech, Pronunciation, and Listening Interest Sections (SPLIS) of International TESOL. In additional to announcements about SPLIS, there are other resources such as "Links for listening," which connects with a wide variety of listening sites.

The Internet TESL Journal's ESL: Listening Page (http://iteslj.org/links/ESL/Listening/)

This provides links to a wide variety of sites. Some of the sites are specifically designed for ESL/EFL students and others are not. It divides the sites into those requiring RealAudio, those with downloadable MP3 files, and those that are podcasts.

References

Bailey, K.M. 2005. *Practical English Language Teaching: Speaking.* New York, NY: McGraw-Hill.

Barnard, R. 1998. *Good News, Bad News.* New York, NY: Oxford University Press.

Brindley, G. 2003. Classroom-based Assessment. In D. Nunan (ed.) *Practical English Language Teaching.* New York, NY: McGraw-Hill, 309-328.

Freeman, D., K. Graves, and L. Lee. 2005. *ICON 1.* New York, NY: McGraw-Hill ESL/ELT.

Helgesen, M. 2003. Listening. In D. Nunan (ed.) *Practical English Language Teaching*. New York, NY: McGraw-Hill, 24.

Helgesen, M. and S. Brown. 1995. *Active Listening 1: Introducing Skills for Understanding*. Cambridge, UK: Cambridge University Press.

Helgesen, M. and S. Brown. 2001. Preface in T. Lesley, *Active Listening Tests*. New York, NY: Cambridge University Press.

Nunan, D. 2003. *Listen In, Book 3* (2nd ed.). Boston, MA: Thomson Heinle.

Peterson, P.W. 2001. Skills and strategies for proficient listening. In M. Celce-Murcia (ed.) *Teaching English as a Second or Foreign Language*. Boston, MA: Heinle & Heinle.

Richards, J.C. and R. Schmidt. 2002. *Longman Dictionary of Language Teaching and Applied Linguistics*. London, UK: Longman.

Richards, J.C. 1990. *The Language Teaching Matrix*. Cambridge, MA: Cambridge University Press.

Rost, M. 2002. *Teaching and Researching Listening*. Harlow, UK: Pearson Education/Longman.

Rubin, J. An Overview to "A Guide for the Teaching of Second Language Listening." In D. Mendelsohn and J. Rubin. 1995. *A Guide for the Teaching of Second Language Listening*. San Diego, CA: Dominie Press.

Rumelhart, D.E. 1977. Toward an interactive model of reading. In S. Dornic (ed.) *Attention and Performance*. VI. Hillsdale, NJ: Erlbaum.

Stein, B.S. and U. Albridge. 1978. The role of conceptual frameworks in prose comprehension and recall. Mimeo. Vanderbilt University, Nashville.

Ur, P. 1984. *Teaching Listening Comprehension*. Cambridge, MA: Cambridge University Press.

Chapter **Two**

Listening for beginning level learners

At the end of the chapter, you should be able to:

Goals

✔ **describe** characteristics of beginning learners.

✔ **explain** the difference between comprehension questions and tasks.

✔ **identify** characteristics you consider important in tasks.

✔ **identify** different levels at which information can be comprehended.

✔ **recognize** principles of teaching beginners.

✔ **understand** ways that spoken and written language differ.

✔ **recognize** different listening tasks and the types of comprehension they require.

1. Introduction

In this chapter, we will begin to develop a task-based model of teaching listening. While doing so, we will focus on the needs of beginning level learners. We will see throughout the book that many of the principles involved and the tasks used for teaching one level of learner can be applied to other levels. We'll also point out tasks and materials that are particularly well suited to one level or another. In the first section, we'll define some words that we'll use throughout the chapter. Next, we'll look at the nature of tasks—language learning activities. We'll then consider three key principles that make teaching and learning how to listen more effective. Following this, we'll look at examples and classroom applications of task-based listening practice. Finally, we'll consider assessment for beginning learners.

What is a beginning level listener? The American Council on the Teaching of Foreign Languages (ACTFL) is a professional organization of foreign language teachers in the United States. It has done extensive work in testing and assessment and has been especially influential in helping determine definitions for student proficiency levels (beginning, intermediate, advanced). ACTFL defines a beginning level listener as someone who:

- understands isolated words and short sentences, especially in a clear context such as the immediate physical setting or requests for personal information.
- comprehends high-frequency words and formulas like greetings *(How are you doing?)*, apologies *(I'm sorry.)*, and questions *(Where are you from?)*.
- may require long pauses for assimilation.
- may require repetition, rephrasing, and/or a slowed rate of speech for comprehension.

Reflection

Have you ever been in a situation where you had to listen in a second or foreign language?

1. Think about the time(s) you did this when you were a beginning learner. What things were easy to do? What was difficult? What kinds of situations were you in when things were easy/difficult? Who were you talking to? What were you talking about? What caused the differences between listening that were easy/difficult?

2. How do the ideas from the ACTFL guidelines compare to what you experienced as a beginning listener?

Share your answers with a classmate or colleague.

While the beginning/intermediate/advanced level distinction is useful when discussing language learners, there are several factors that are common to all levels that have to be taken into account.

- **Receptive vs. productive skills**. In Chapter 1, we pointed out that listening is a **receptive skill**. As such, people can understand far more than they can produce. Notice that the ACTFL guidelines recognize this. They use words like *understand* and *comprehend* rather than productive verbs like *explain*, *write*, or *summarize*. This has important implications for our teaching, both in realizing that students can understand more than they can say and also in making sure it is possible for them to respond in a way that demonstrates their understanding without demanding they demonstrate in a way that requires more productive language than they have.
- **Topic and schema**. We introduced the concept of **schema** or background knowledge in Chapter 1. Schemata affect our level of understanding as well. Because you are reading this book, as authors we can assume that you are interested in language teaching. Whether you are teaching now or preparing to be a teacher later, we can assume a certain amount of shared knowledge and interest between you, as a reader, and us, as the writers. That knowledge makes it easier for you to understand what we are writing. If we were suddenly to switch to a topic you don't know anything about—say nuclear physics or Australian Aboriginal dot painting—it would be much harder to understand even if the language was at the same level as when we are writing about teaching and learning. Why? The lack of schemata. In the same way, the topics your learners listen to impact their level of understanding.
- **True vs. false beginners**. In English teaching, we often distinguish between the **ESL (English as a Second Language)** world and the **EFL (English as a Foreign Language)** world. ESL teaching situations are in countries where English is used either as the national language or used daily as a **lingua franca** (a common language in a country that has many languages, ethnic groups, etc. India, Singapore, and Kenya are common examples). EFL teaching situations are where English is taught as a school subject but where actual use of English outside the class is limited. In EFL situations, many learners are false beginners—they have learned a lot of language, especially vocabulary and grammar, but are often unable to use it to express themselves. Because of what we said about listening being a receptive skill, we need to think about ways to help false beginners use what they have learned. This is in contrast to true beginners who have never studied English before.

2. Syllabus design issues

Teaching, not testing

Most of the time, we want to be helping learners improve their listening skills, not just testing them. A key to achieving this goal is to adopt a task-based approach.

Action

Traditionally, language lessons have been filled with comprehension questions. Comprehension questions are troublesome for several reasons. To demonstrate the problem, try the following exercise based on a single sentence of nonsense words.

The glorfs drebbled quarfly.

1. (grammar analysis) In the sentence above, underline the subject and circle the verb.

2. What part of speech is *quarfly*?

3. What did the *glorfs* do?

4. How did they do it?

4. quarfly

Answers: 1. underline *glorfs*, circle *drebbled*.   **2.** adverb   **3.** They drebbled.

Most people are able to answer all the items in the Action box above correctly—which may be strange since the sentence doesn't actually mean anything. This highlights one of the major flaws with comprehension questions. They tend to test one type of comprehension, often out of context. In the case of questions about a listening text, if learners get the answers wrong, you don't know if it is because they didn't understand what they heard, they didn't understand the questions, they know the answers but don't know how to say or write their answers in English, or they understood at the time but forgot by the time they had to write their answers.

It is now assumed to be common knowledge in language teaching that comprehension questions are not the best tool for finding out what learners understand, but of course, as teachers we need to know what our students understand. One solution, one we think is the best one, is tasks. Richards and Renandya (2002) define a **task** as: "an activity which learners carry out using their available language resources and leading to a real outcome."

The "real outcome" is a key to a task—there needs to be a clear goal. A good rule of thumb for identifying a task is that an activity only has a task if learners know when they've finished it. Another way to say this is that tasks necessarily have a focus that is not on language, but on getting something done—what Nunan (2004) calls a "non-linguistic outcome."

Go back to the list of things you identified in the Reflection box in Chapter 1 on page 2. Some things were tasks that required responses. Some weren't. For example, if you heard birds singing, you probably didn't actually need to do anything in response. On the other hand, if you heard the telephone ring, you probably had to do something—answer it.

1. Which did you have to make some kind of response to?

2. Do these qualify as "tasks" in your mind? How are they similar to or different from those you might see in a classroom?

Share your answers with a classmate or colleague.

Current textbooks feature a wide variety of tasks. Learners listen and check off correct answers, identify pictures/words, or in some way react to what they hear. Generally, the learners do those tasks in "real-time"—that is, while they listen. For this reason, it is important that the task is fairly simple, especially at the beginning levels. If the learners have to do a lot of writing to answer a question, for example, they will be unable to concentrate on listening as they are writing. A list of learning tasks appears in Appendix 1 on pages 158–161.

Generally, but not always, the tasks in most textbooks are based on meaning. At the simplest levels, students may be asked to identify which picture is being talked about or write a phone number they hear. This doesn't mean that "old-fashioned" tasks that focus on grammar or vocabulary aren't useful. They are. But the discussion of **top-down** and **bottom-up processing** in Chapter 1 (page 6) showed that teachers need to encourage processing in both directions. Bottom-up processing of items like form and vocabulary should happen in the overall context of a situation. So, for example, you might have a first task where learners identify the main idea or the sequence of a series of events, then a follow-up task where learners hear the same recording and identify verbs used. Actually, this type of exercise is about meaning, too. It is just that the students are thinking about the meaning of the grammar rather than the meaning of the content.

Reflection

Think about your experience as a language learner or teacher.

1. How many different types of tasks do you remember using in listening classes?

2. What seemed important or useful about the tasks you use(d)?

3. Look at Appendix 1, page 158, which is a list of possible listening tasks. Which do you already know? If you are teaching now, you might want to choose a few that you would like to try.

Share your answers with a classmate or colleague.

Action

1. Look at the questionnaire below. Based on your experience as a learner (of language and other things) and any experience you have teaching (informal as well as formal), how important do you think the following items are?

Questionnaire on the "Good" Learning Task

What do you believe?

Circle the appropriate number following each of the criteria below according to the following scale:

0 – This is not a characteristic of a good task.
1 – This characteristic may be present, but is optional.
2 – This characteristic is reasonably important.
3 – This characteristic is extremely important.
4 – This characteristic is essential.

Good learning tasks should:

1. enable learners to manipulate and practice specific features of language.   0 1 2 3 4

2. allow learners to rehearse, in class, communicative skills they will need in the real world.   0 1 2 3 4

3. activate psychological/psycholinguistic processes of learning (e.g., should make learners think).   0 1 2 3 4

4. be suitable for mixed ability groups.   0 1 2 3 4

5. involve learners in solving a problem, coming to a conclusion.   0 1 2 3 4

6. be based on authentic or naturalistic source material.	0	1	2	3	4
7. involve learners in sharing information.	0	1	2	3	4
8. require the use of more than one macroskill (e.g., *listening* plus *reading* or *speaking*).	0	1	2	3	4
9. allow learners to think and talk about language and learning.	0	1	2	3	4
10. promote skills in learning how to learn.	0	1	2	3	4
11. have clear objectives stating what learners will be able to do as a result of taking part in the task.	0	1	2	3	4
12. utilize the community as a resource.	0	1	2	3	4
13. give learners a choice in what they do and the order in which they do it.	0	1	2	3	4
14. involve learners in risk-taking.	0	1	2	3	4
15. require learners to rehearse, rewrite, and polish initial efforts.	0	1	2	3	4
16. enable learners to share in the planning and development of the task.	0	1	2	3	4
17. have built into them a means of evaluating the success or otherwise of the task.	0	1	2	3	4
18. be easy to set up and explain to the students.*	0	1	2	3	4

(Nunan 2004, pp. 169–170)
*Item 18 did not appear in the original questionnaire, nor do the examples.

2. Choose the five most important characteristics of a task. If you are doing this activity with a class, it can be useful to compare your results with those of other people. What did you think was important? Why did other people answer differently?

3. Did the tasks you identified in the Reflection box on page 30 include the characteristics you believe are important?

Levels of processing

We've suggested that tasks are a key to teaching listening. In the previous chapter, we talked about learner purpose (specific information, gist, inference) and **direction of processing** (top-down and bottom-up). To that mix, we need to add the idea of "levels of processing."

Woody Allen once joked that he had taken a speed-reading course, and it worked. "Yesterday I read *War and Peace* in two hours... It's about some Russians." He may have read the book, but he wasn't processing very deeply.

There are several ways to look at how deeply we think about what we hear. Figure 1 is one such way.

5. Appreciation (highest level)
Students give an emotional or image-based response.

4. Evaluation
Students make judgments in light of the material.

3. Inference
Students respond to information that is implied but not directly stated.

2. Reorganization
Students organize or order the information a different way than it was presented.

1. Literal (lowest level)
Students identify information directly stated.

Figure 1: Barrett's taxonomy of levels of comprehension (1965)

Note that you shouldn't assume that beginning learners start at the lowest level and move up the scale as they get more proficient in listening (and therefore put off the highest level until they're advanced learners). A beginning level student is capable of appreciation, of giving an emotional response, if the language and the task are properly selected by the teacher.

Although Barrett's taxonomy was originally written to focus on reading comprehension, the levels hold true for listening as well. We'll look more at specific examples of these different levels in Section 5 of this chapter. For now it is enough to notice that learners clearly have to think more deeply during some tasks than others. It is also interesting to notice that literal comprehension, the type that is certainly most common in textbook questions and tasks, tests understanding at the lowest level.

3. Principles for teaching listening to beginning learners

As we've said, most principles of teaching beginning learners apply to intermediate and advanced learners as well. The principles in this section are probably the most basic for teaching listening generally, so we'll take them up first.

1. Be aware of the goal of your task.

You can't hit a target if you don't know where it is. If tasks require a clear outcome, then it follows that learners need to be aware of what the goal is before they begin the activity.

This should be obvious, but sometimes it isn't. Think of how often you've seen books that give students a text to read or listen to, followed by a series of questions. We've already pointed out the limitations of comprehension questions, but if learners have to deal with them, at least they should know the questions before they listen. If they don't, they really don't know what they are listening for. And in the real world, you almost always know why you're listening.

In the classroom, keeping the students' goal in focus can be as simple as pointing it out to them. For example, you might say, "Listen to the dialogue and write down the phone number the speaker says." It is also useful to give the learners time to look over the page or activity. They should certainly read the instructions. If there are pictures, they can look at them and see how many things they know how to describe in English. If there are questions or other written information, they should read it and think about possible answers. All of this is useful in "activating schema." When learners take time at the beginning of a task to rehearse, to think about and plan what they're going to do, they are usually more successful at the task. If they're going to be speaking, taking this additional planning time is more likely to lead to richer, more complex language. They increase their meaning-focused **fluency**. Interestingly, there are often increases in their **accuracy** as well (Skehan and Foster, 1997).

2. Use a variety of tasks.

Learners need to become comfortable with a variety of tasks. In part this is because we listen to different things in different ways. Listening to the news to catch the gist is very different than needing to catch someone's phone number or a homework assignment. Naturally, the tasks we do to practice each will need to be different as well.

There is another, very important reason for task variety. Howard (2000, p. 510) talks about the brain's need for variety: "Our sensory receptors become aroused when a new stimulus begins, but if the new stimulus continues without variation in quality or quantity, our sensory receptors shut down from their aroused state, becoming habituated, or accustomed, to the monotonous stimulus. A change in the quality or quantity of the stimulus will arouse the receptors again. This is why, for example, it is hard to pay attention to someone who speaks in a monotone. It is also why people often add salt, pepper, or other seasoning after a few bites."

Dörnyei (2001, p. 73) expands on this need to avoid habituation: "Monotony is inversely related to variety. In order to break monotony, we need to vary as many aspects of the learning process as possible. First and foremost are the *language tasks*."

Look again at Appendix 1 (pages 158–161) and notice the variety of tasks that are possible.

Action

1. Think about the language tasks you identified in the Reflection box on page 30. Choose two or three that were not very interesting. Look again at the list of tasks in Appendix 1. How could you revise the uninteresting tasks to improve them—or at least make them different?

Share your answer with a classmate or colleague.

Reflection

When teaching listening, we are dealing with the spoken language. Spoken language is different than written language.

1. Think about your own experience in your native language. In what ways do you speak differently than you write?

2. How might these differences make it easier for a listener to understand the language? How might they make it more difficult?

3. If you have experience in a foreign or second language, how do the differences affect your ability to understand? How did those differences affect your ability when you were first learning the language?

Share your answers with a classmate or colleague.

3. Be aware of the difference between spoken and written language.

One of the biggest differences between spoken and written language is that, in informal conversation, we usually don't speak in sentences. We speak in short phrases called **idea units**. Buck (2001) points out that these idea units are "strung together in a rather loose way, often connected more by the coherence of the ideas than by any formal grammatical relationship. The vocabulary and the grammar also tend to be far more colloquial and much less formal" (p. 9). Buck goes on to identify other differences in spoken versus written English. The following is our summary of Buck's key points.

- **Spoken** language is redundant. We often repeat ideas, saying the same thing more than once. (The last two sentences are an example of this in that a single idea was stated three times.)
- **Spoken** language is not always fluent. When we are making up what we say as we go along, there is not only repetition but also hesitations and **false starts** where we begin to say something and then change it. Experts disagree on the effects of false starts. Ur (1984) suggests these factors can give listeners more time to work out what the speaker means. Bowen and Marks (1994) counter that, while that might be true for proficient listeners, it can confuse beginning learners.
- **Spoken** language often has more non-standard features like slang and colloquialisms. For example a few years ago, in Hip Hop culture, words like "bling" (expensive jewelry) and "dis" (to disrespect someone) were common in spoken language but less likely to be used in written language, unless, of course, the writing was supposed to reflect spoken form. Written English is more formal and "correct."
- **Spoken** language is more personal, using phrases like "I think…" and "I mean…" It shows more emotion and is less precise than written language.
- **Spoken** language also contains more references to things that are not stated directly in the text (Flowerdew and Miller, 2005).
- **Spoken** language includes **prosody**—sound characteristics such as stress, intonation, loudness, pitch, and duration of syllables.

Action

Of course, the above list contains generalizations. In reality, spoken versus written language is more of a continuum. To see where things fit, try this task from Flowerdew and Miller (2005).

On a separate piece of paper, reproduce the continuum of spokenness and writtenness shown below. Next, place the following genres on the scale by drawing lines from the genre to the appropriate place on the continuum.

Compare your continuum with a classmate or colleague.

| spokenness | | writtenness |

casual conversation	university lecture	academic research article
school textbook	shopping list	postcard
political speech	email message	church service
press conference	telephone	travel reservation
radio news		

Since spoken language is so different from written language, it is important we give students experience in listening to spoken language rather than recordings of written text. Often this can make the text challenging. One strategy is to adjust the task. In the Gimpo Airport segment in Chapter 1 (page 14), you saw an example of making a difficult text accessible by having a very focused task. This leads us to our next principle.

4. Build on success.

It is often said that *success breeds success*. To help our students become successful listeners, we need to give them successful experiences. Dörnyei (2001) suggests three ways to do just that:

- Provide multiple opportunities for success in the language class.
- Adjust the difficulty level of the tasks to match the students' abilities and counterbalance demanding tasks with manageable ones.
- Design tests that focus on what learners can do rather than what they cannot do, and also include improvement options.

Action

At times, a task or the recording from the textbook you are using may be too difficult for at least some of your learners.

1. If you have faced overly difficult tasks as a teacher or as a learner, what did you do?

2. If you were asked to teach a lesson that contained overly difficult listening tasks for your students, what would you do? With a partner come up with five ways you could help your students be successful with the lesson.

Here are some tricks that will help learners deal with difficult tasks.

1. Do a pre-listening warm-up activity to remind them of content and vocabulary they will need (schema activation).
2. Have learners do a task in pairs. That way, they often share what they did understand instead of worrying about what they missed.
3. Do a *micro-task* before the main task.
   - Brainstorm words likely to be in the listening text. When your learners listen, have them raise their hands when they hear one of the words. This shows recognition and is a cue for other learners.
   - Give a list of events or items that will be mentioned in the listening text. Then have students listen and identify the sequence.
   - As students listen, pause the recording to give them time to think and process what they hear.

- If the listening is a **cloze activity** in which students listen and write missing words in a reading passage, have the learners read the passage first. They may want to guess at the words or types of words they expect to hear.

4. Give students a copy of the script and have them read it. Then ask them to put the script away and listen to the text. After they listen, have them take their scripts back out. The students then listen and underline a key feature (e.g., the information that contained the answers, a certain grammatical form, etc.).

5. Have students choose their own style of review. After doing a task and checking it, play the text again. Invite the students to choose their own level for review.
   - Those who found it very difficult watch you. As you play the recording, point to the answers on the board or an overhead projector as they are mentioned.
   - Those who found it of average difficulty look at their books. They try to hear the answers and touch them as they do so.
   - Those who found it easy close their eyes. As they listen, they "watch the movie in their minds."

4. Tasks and materials

The purpose of this section is to look at tasks and materials that are used in the classroom. While the range of possible listening tasks is nearly endless, we will look at six general categories that are useful with beginning learners.

1. pre-listening warm-up activities
2. listening for specific information/literal comprehension
3. listening for gist/reorganization
4. inferencing
5. listening and making evaluations
6. appreciation

The first, pre-listening warm-ups, are essential for schema activation mentioned earlier. You may have already noticed that the others on this list parallel the levels of comprehension categories mentioned earlier. While there are many ways to organize listening tasks, we find that tying them to the different levels at which one tries to understand things is a good way to make sure our students get experience listening at all the levels.

Pre-listening warm-ups

Earlier we emphasized the importance of doing a pre-listening warm-up to activate learners' schemata. This is important in building a successful orientation. It is also very practical for classroom management since it helps learners focus, gets them "thinking in the right direction," and is often an interactive task where they work with each other.

Action

Below are three examples from leading beginning level textbooks. All three examples are warm-up activities that lead into listening tasks. They all deal with the same language function: talking about schedules.

As you look at them, notice:
- how new vocabulary, grammar, and **functional phrases** are introduced or how the language the students already know is activated.
- how the task is personalized.
- what you like or dislike about each one.

Example 1

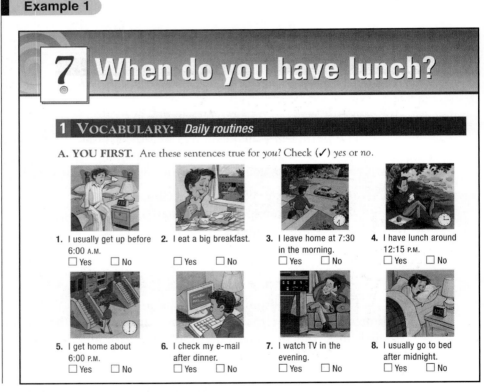

Icon Intro (Freeman, Graves, and Lee, 2005, p. 44)

Example 2

Listen in 1 (Nunan, 2003, p. 56)

Example 3

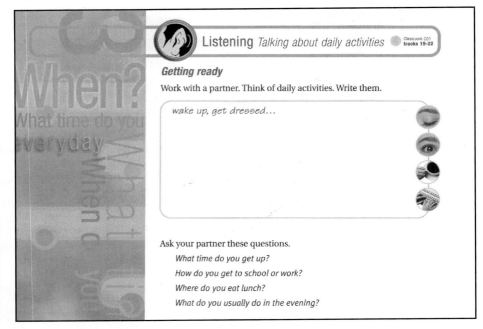

English Firsthand 1 (Helgesen, Brown, and Mandeville, 2004, p. 28)

As important as warm-ups are for schema activation, we need to keep in mind a warning from Buck (1995, pp. 125–126): "If you look at some listening textbooks, they provide twenty minutes of pre-listening activities for about three minutes of listening practice. This is unbalanced. We need pre-listening activities to do two things: provide a context for interpretation and activate the background knowledge which will help interpretation. Give them enough to do that, and then let them listen."

Examples 1, 2, and 3 show a range of pre-listening activities. Example 1 (page 38) presents the sentences and illustrates the target vocabulary next to pictures. The learners are being taught new vocabulary. Example 2 (page 39) provides the vocabulary but asks the learners to reorganize the information by matching it to the correct picture. This assumes learners have some knowledge of the vocabulary. Example 3 assumes that the learners already know a lot of English vocabulary and challenges them to see how much they can produce. The kind of pre-listening activity that is used has something to do with the level of the students. In books for true beginners, vocabulary is nearly always taught. In books for false beginners, the authors assume a substantial amount of known information and provide ways for learners to access or remember it.

All three examples also **personalize** the activity, but in different ways. Example 1 starts with simple *yes/no* questions about the learners' own routines.

Then it moves into a classic personalized activity called "Find someone who" (not shown). Learners ask the questions and try to find someone who can say *yes*. This is a useful example of an activity that, while it involves speaking, is very much a listening activity as well. Learners need to pay attention to their partners in order to complete the task.

Example 2 is personalized by having learners write more sentences about the character in the book. The sentences are based on the students' imagination.

Example 3 asks for daily activities. These come from the learners' personal lives and experiences. Then they work in pairs, asking questions about their partner's routines.

In Chapter 1, we talked about types of listening, including specific information, gist, and inference. In this chapter, we present levels of processing: literal, reorganization, inference, evaluation, and appreciation. While these lists are not the same thing, there is clearly some overlap between the two.

Action

We hope you will take the time to actually listen to the samples on the PELT Listening audio program. Of course, it would be faster to just read over the scripts found in Appendix 2 (pages 162–168), but when you actually listen, your experience is closer to that of the students so you are more likely to understand things the way they would.

As you listen to the tracks for Examples 4 (page 42) and 5 (page 44), think about how students who are learning would experience them. Make notes, perhaps in the margins of the pages, about what you notice.

- Would the exercises be easy? Difficult? Too easy? Too difficult?
- Would they be of interest? Would learners find them practical and useful?
- The disembodied voice of a recording is always harder to understand than a person saying the same thing in person. The speaker doesn't interact with the listener and doesn't get the feedback that is typical in face-to-face conversation. One textbook editor we know encourages actors to project at 110% to make up for the flatness of a recording. Most of the recordings were made in recording studios using professional actors. They all attempt to sound natural. Some succeed better than others. What makes a recording seem natural?
- Think about how these samples do (or don't!) reflect the ideas and principles in this book.
- How do they fit with your beliefs as a teacher?
- Which would you like to teach? Why?

Listening for specific information/literal processing

Listening for specific information is one of the most common tasks in the listening classroom. Listening for specifics isn't limited to **literal processing**, but often they go together. While literal understanding is the lowest level of processing, it doesn't mean it is unimportant. Much of the information we get day-to-day we get though literal processing.

Audio

Example 4

CD Track 7

▷**Before You Listen**

Work with your partner. Arrange the sentences to make a conversation between a customer and a waiter in a coffee shop. The first one is done for you.

.... Anything else sir?
.... Certainly sir. Coming right up.
__1__ Are you ready to order, sir?
.... Cream and sugar?
.... Thank you.
.... Yes, please. I'd like a cup of coffee.
.... Just black's fine.
.... And a piece of toast.

Now say the dialogue with your partner. Take turns to be the customer and the waiter/waitress.

Look at the items in *Let's Start!* again. Change the dialogue and order some more food and drink.

▷**Let's Listen!**

Listen to three conversations. Look at the pictures. Write the letter of the order next to the number of the conversation.

ⓐ ⓑ ⓒ

ⓓ ⓔ

ⓕ

Conversation 1 ....
Conversation 2 ....
Conversation 3 ....

Check your answers with your partner.

⁝ Listen Again

Listen to the conversations again. Circle *F* if the waiter asks a question only about the food. Circle *D* if the waiter asks a question only about the drink. Circle *B* if the waiter asks a question about both the food and the drink.

Conversation 1	F	D	B
Conversation 2	F	D	B
Conversation 3	F	D	B

Check your answers with your partner.

⁝ Listening Clinic One: Strong or Weak?

Words are stressed when they are important. Words are not stressed when they are not important.

Examples	
	A: A cup of coffee and a donut.
	B: A cup of coffee. Anything else?
	A: And a donut.

Listen to the dialogue. Draw a slash (/) through the words: *and*, *a* and *of* where they are spoken *weakly*.

A: Can I help you?
B: Yes, I'd like a piece of cheesecake.
A: Large, or small?
B: Small please. And a cup of coffee.
A: A piece of cheesecake and a cup of coffee.
B: That's right.

Check your answers with your partner. Now say the dialogue together.

Top-Up Listening 1 (Cleary, Holden, and Cooney, 2003, pp. 22–23)

When you listened to Example 4, you probably noticed that there was a lot of redundancy. The restaurant server repeated the customer's order. You probably also noticed informal forms (*'kay* for OK) and hesitation markers like *Mmm* and *Um*. These reflect spoken language.

Notice also that there are six pictures but only three conversations. The exercise was designed this way so that learners have to listen all the way to the end of the task rather than finding the answer by choosing the item that hasn't been chosen yet.

The second time the recording is played, the learners listen for different information. This is useful in helping learners get a deeper understanding of the text without simply playing the recording several times. It also increases task awareness since they notice they are listening to the same thing for different reasons.

Notice the "Listening Clinic" task. Students here are paying attention to the actual language and pronunciation, not just the overall meaning. This is an example of a bottom-up **FonF (Focus on Form)** task, but notice that it is taking place within the context of the overall meaning of the conversation.

Another traditional technique often used with beginners, one that focuses on literal comprehension and forms of language, is **TPR (Total Physical Response)**. In TPR, the teacher, or one of the learners, gives commands (*Stand up. Walk to the door*, etc.) that learners follow. In following the commands, learners are focusing on specific words.

Listening for gist/reorganization

Again, **gist listening** can take many forms. Reorganizing information is simply one of them. A common reorganizing task is to have learners listen to a segment and number pictures or items, based on what they hear.

Audio

Example 5

CD Track 8

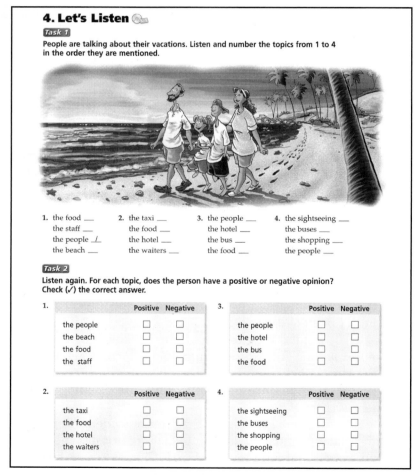

Developing Tactics in Listening (Richards, 2003, p. 48)

Listen to the text for Example 5. Notice that the first item has been completed as a model. This simple technique can be very useful in demonstrating to learners what they need to do. If learners have difficulty with the task, try pausing the recording after each topic to give learners a chance to think and write their answers. The second task, listening for the speakers' opinions, is a good example of giving learners a second chance to hear a segment, this time with a different purpose.

Inferencing

Inferencing is somewhat different than other types of listening, in that it often happens in the middle of listening tasks designed for some other purpose. A person might be listening for specifics or for gist, but if the speaker says things indirectly or happens to use vocabulary the listener doesn't know, that listener needs to infer the meaning.

Inferencing is a higher level listening skill. However, it is a mistake to wait until learners are at an intermediate level or above to begin working on it. Indeed, beginning learners lack the large vocabulary and grammatical knowledge that they will have later, so they *need* to "listen between the lines" at their level. Example 6 (page 46) shows how this can be done at a very elementary level. Notice that even though the speakers don't say the name of the food, you are able to understand what they are talking about. As you listen, notice the words that give you the clues.

Example 6

CD Track 9

Audio

LISTENING TASK 1

This tastes great!

Inferring topics

❑ Listen. People are eating different foods. They don't say the names of the foods.
What are they talking about?
Number the pictures (1–6). There are two extra pictures.

☐ pizza   ☐ fish   ☐ sushi (Japanese)

☐ hamburger   [1] ice cream cone   ☐ soup

☐ coffee   ☐ nan (Indian)

Active Listening 1 (Helgesen and Brown, 1995, p. 16)

Having learners notice which words give them clues can be very useful. You might have them work in pairs or small groups. They share their answers and how they arrived at them. This gives weaker learners examples from more successful peers.

At times it is possible to add inference to an activity where it isn't specifically in the material. Sometimes, it is a matter of asking, *How does the character feel? Why do you think so?*

Listening and making evaluations

This does not involve evaluating the student. Rather, it is students making evaluations of what they hear. In Example 7, learners are hearing unusual news stories. They have to decide if the stories could be true or not.

Example 7

CD Track 10

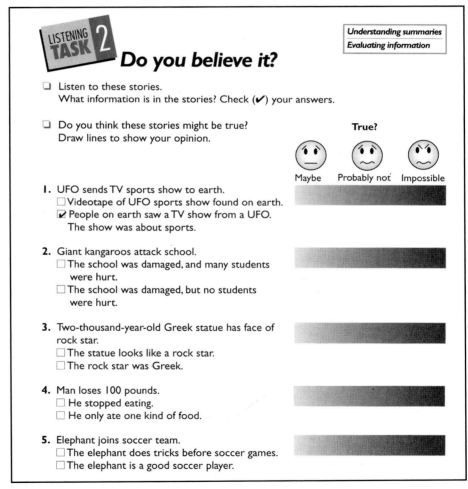

Active Listening 1 (Helgesen and Brown, 1995, pp. 54 and 56)

Evaluation activities are fairly rare in textbooks, especially at the beginning level. The skill is, however, essential to critical thinking. At times, we can add evaluation simply by asking follow-up questions, especially with stories. For example:

- Do you think this story is true? Why or why not?
- Would you have done the same thing as character *X*? Why or why not?

Appreciation

In daily life, listening for pleasure is common for most people. We often do it when we watch TV or listen to music. We are listening to enjoy. It is perhaps ironic that the highest level of comprehension can be accessed through a very simple question: *Did you enjoy the story? Why or why not?*

If a learner can answer these questions it shows understanding, often at a higher level than shown by seemingly more complex tasks. Of course, since listening is receptive and speaking productive, the learners may initially have to give the reasons in their first language, or we may want to structure an activity to give them more support. In Example 8, students hear six short musical cuts (two of which are on Track 11). They imagine they are hearing them on the radio for the first time. They decide what they would do. Then they write one word that describes how the song makes them feel.

Example 8

CD Track 11

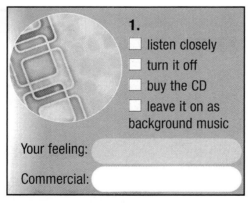

English Firsthand 1 (Helgesen, Brown, and Mandeville, 2004, p. 107)

After doing the appreciative listening, they hear the cuts again. This time they are told the songs are background music to a TV commercial. They imagine the commercial and what it is advertising. Then they discuss their ideas in small groups. This activity is unusual in that the main listening task involves listening to their partners, not just a recording.

We used this example for appreciation since music is so popular with students. Unfortunately, the pleasure and emotion that music can bring is often lost when we use it with lower level tasks like *write the missing words* (literal comprehension). At times, listening to music and stories and just enjoying them is task enough.

An interesting note–during pre-publication piloting of the activity in Example 8, the authors used many different music segments. Segment number one got very high negative ratings from many students. That's the reason it is first. The authors wanted something the learners would feel strongly about to get them thinking about what they do and do not enjoy.

Reflection

- Which of the examples you listened to in this section seemed natural?
- Look over the audio scripts (pages 162–168). How did they succeed or fail to incorporate the features of spoken language?

As you can see, there is a great variety in the types of tasks we can ask learners to do. Providing that variety ensures not only that they listen to many things in different ways, it also lets them understand on different levels.

Action

1. Without looking at the previous pages, which of the example tasks can you list?

2. Why do you think those are the ones you remembered?

Share your answers with a classmate or colleague.

5. Listening in the beginning classroom

Many textbooks have a teacher's manual–also called teacher's edition–which gives invaluable support–usually with step-by-step teaching instructions, extra activities, and tests. In looking at what does, and what can, happen in the classroom, a good place to start is with a teacher's manual.

1. Have you used a teacher's manual? If yes, what did you find useful in the manual? What was not useful to you?

2. Below are some common features of teacher's manuals. How important are they for you? Rate them using the scale below.

0 = I would never use
1 = not important

2 = nice to have but not essential
3 = very important

———— lesson objectives

———— lesson plans

———— alternative ways to teach the textbook tasks

———— scripts for recordings

———— teacher's scripts (what the teacher should say)

———— answer keys

———— grammar, vocabulary notes

———— culture notes

———— extra "out of the book" activities

3. What else should a teacher's manual have?

Share your answers with a classmate or colleague.

Example 9 is the pages from the teacher's manual that goes with Example 3 (page 40).

Example 9

unit 3 When do you start?

Unit overview
Objective: Students will talk about routines and how often people do things.
Functions: Talking about routines and plans
Grammar: Frequency and time adverbials
Vocabulary themes: Daily activities
Classroom language: I don't understand.
Language planning: Answering personal questions, choosing topics, preparing responses

Listening Talking ab[...]

In brief
The students [...]
common daily [...]
In the *First Listening* [...]
schedules.
In the *Second Listeni[...]*
tion.
In *About You*, they ar[...]
routines.

Getting Ready

Lesson plan
❶ T: *Look at page 28.* [...]
talk about their daily [...]
❷ ↑↑ T: *Look at "Get[...]*
Think of daily activiti[...]*
(Try Option ♦, next [...]
❸ Allow time for lear[...]
work, circulate and h[...]
❹ ↑↑ T: *Now ask yo[...]*
time for learners to d[...]
Continue with the re[...]
next page.

Optional warm-up ac[...]

Frequency circle gar[...]
Preparation: You'll n[...]
(or balled-up piece o[...]
eight students.
Procedure: On the cl[...]
I always ____ (almos[...]
ly ever, never)
Students work in gro[...]
cle. One begins by sa[...]
of the frequency adv[...]
pro wrestling on TV). [...]
ball/animal to some[...]
catches it continues [...]
and adding her own [...]
wrestling on TV. I aln[...]
Saturday night). Tha[...]
new. The third studer[...]

Listening Tasks
Classroom CD1, tracks 20-22 Self-Study CD, tracks 13-15

Lesson plan
(If your students find listening very challenging, try Option ♦, below.)
❶ ♀ ↑↑ T: *Look at page 29. First listening. People are talking about their daily schedule. Listen. Number the pictures 1–4. Write the time of day next to each picture.* Play the *First Listening* recording. Gesture for students to write their answers. You may want to pause within each recording to give students more time to think and answer.
❷ Check the answers to *First Listening* by asking students the questions. T: *Alan goes jogging. When does he do that?* (A: in the morning.)
❸ ♀ ↑↑ T: *Second listening. Listen again. Write extra information next to each picture.* Play the recording again. Gesture for students to write extra information. (Try Option ♣, below.)
❹ Check as in step 2.
❺ ♀ T: *About you. Listen. Answer the questions about yourself.* Play the *About you* recording. (Classroom CD1, track 22; Self-Study CD, track 15) You may need to pause between items to give students enough time to write.
❻ Check by having students compare with a partner. (Try Option ♥, below.)

Options and variations

♦ **Extra preparation listening warm-up**
Students work in pairs. Before they listen, they look at the eight small pictures on page 29. They write or say what they think is happening in each picture.
♣ As an example of getting extra information, you may want to stop the recording after the first bit (after *I like to stay in shape*) and have a few learners say what they caught (*he jogs for 30 minutes, he eats a light breakfast, etc.*).
♥ Once they know the answers, consider playing the recording again. Students can follow in their books or close their eyes and imagine the conversation.

Learner power
The second task encourages students to go beyond the basic task and to notice other information they *did* understand. Note that this is a very flexible task. If you are ever in a situation where you want to play a recording again but the students have already done the book tasks, you can add this as a new task.

Language notes
movie junkie = someone "addicted" to movies (likes movies very much)

T29

Audio script: Listening tasks

Number 1. This is Alan. Classroom CD1, track 20 Self-Study CD, track 13
Interviewer: Hi, Alan. Could you tell us what you do during a typical day?
Alan: OK, sure. Let's see. Well, I almost always get up at 6:45. Then I usually jog for 30 minutes or so – I like to stay in shape – and I eat a light breakfast and take the train to my office. I usually get there around 8:30.
Interviewer: And, where do you work?
Alan: At Lynch-Hawkins, the law firm downtown.
Interviewer: Hmm. And then, about lunch time... What do you usually do for lunch?
Alan: Lunch? Well, I usually eat quickly at Salad Days over on Front and Green Street. It's a health food restaurant near the office.
Interviewer: Oh, right. And then, after work...?
Alan: After work... I usually get home between 6:00 and 6:30. And when I get home, I fix dinner. Oh, I love cooking and I try to make a lot of new things.
Interviewer: Hmm. And then, how about after dinner? What do you usually do?
Alan: Oh, after dinner? Nothing special. I usually just stay home. I'm a movie junkie and I like to watch old movies on the ShowTime cable channel.

Number 2. This is Lynn. Classroom CD1, track 21 Self-Study CD, track 14
Interviewer: Hi, Lynn. Can you tell us something about what you do during a typical day?
Lynn: Sure. Um, I work at the post office. I have to start at 6 a.m. so I always get up around 5:00. I shower, have breakfast, and catch the 5:45 bus to the post office. We live really close, so it just takes 10 or 15 minutes.
Interviewer: What do you do for lunch?
Lynn: Well, I have a short lunch break, from 11:00 to 11:30, so I usually just bring a sandwich from home and eat that.
Interviewer: What time do you finish work?
Lynn: I finish work at three in the afternoon. So I get home early – a little after three. I love that because I'm home when my two kids, Joey and Erica, get back from school. So between 3:00 and 6:00, I get to play with my kids and make dinner, and we all eat dinner together.
Interviewer: How about after dinner? What do you do?
Lynn: Well, you know, I usually help the kids with their homework. I read to them, get them ready for bed. And one night a week...

About you Classroom CD1, track 22 Self-Study CD, track 15
Listen. Answer the questions about yourself.
1. What time do you usually get up?
2. What do you usually do for lunch?
3. What do you like to do after school or work?
4. What do you usually do on weekends?
5. How often do you study English – outside of class?

Listening answer key on page T32

English Firsthand 1 Teacher's Manual (Helgesen, Brown, and Mandeville, 2004, pp.T28–T29)

1. Look at Example 9 on page 51. What features you identified as useful in the Action box on page 50 can you find? Which are missing?

2. Can you find other features you hadn't thought of?

3. Imagine you are teaching the page to learners who find listening difficult. What advice does the manual give?

4. Read through the lesson plan on page 51. Notice the way the teacher's script gives the instructions.

A teacher's manual is very different than other types of books. No one reads an entire manual from beginning to end. Indeed, most teachers don't even read the lesson straight through. Different teachers have different needs. Variables include:

- Native English Speaking Teachers (NESTs) & Non-NESTs
- the amount of experience the teacher has
- the amount of formal training the teacher has
- the amount of planning time available/used
- the level, size, and needs of a particular class

There are several features of a teacher's manual that we think are worth noting, especially since they may not be obvious at first.

First off, the manual in Example 9 includes the teacher's script. Some people assume that it is intended for non-native speakers. Actually, the real intention is for teachers (native or non-native) who are new. It is very easy for inexperienced teachers, especially ones who are a bit nervous, to talk too much. They give instructions that are not particularly thought out, either in terms of language or the concrete steps of the task. The result is something like this:

OK,sowe'regoingtodosomelisteningso,um,canyou,like,openyourbookstopage29andwhatwehaveis,umthisisAlan,Alan.Yeah,andhe'sgoingtotalkabouthis,youknow,whathedoeseveryday.

The result is a confused class of students. Notice that the teacher's script in Example 9 is written in very short sentences. They are either simple, declarative sentences *(People are talking about their daily schedule.)* or imperative sentences *(Listen. Number the pictures 1–4. Write the time of day next to each picture.).*

These short, clear instructions are easier for students to follow. There is a second, perhaps less obvious purpose. It supports teachers who really haven't planned their lesson but makes it easy to find what to say. We obviously don't recommend not planning but know it sometimes happens. Having a script can be a useful place to start when "winging" a class.

Another bonus of a good teacher's manual is that the basic lesson plan has options and variations. The teacher's manual's authors assume that most beginning teachers are more likely to follow the very basic lesson plan. Variations give more experienced teachers support.

Finally, many teacher's manuals give optional warm-up activities. Most textbook authors assume that teachers do not teach their books straight through, covering one page, then the next, then the next. It is useful for teachers to get the learners out of the books regularly. This is necessary both for maintaining interest and variety as well as providing the students with different experiences—we don't spend all of our lives on controlled, textbook conversations and activities.

We will go into greater depth about lesson planning in Chapter 3. For now, it is useful simply to notice where listening fits into this overall lesson plan. Let's look again at Example 9 (page 51).

The "Getting Ready" activity is the warm-up. It serves to activate the language the learners already know. It also personalizes the task. This can either be the warm-up for the entire class, or the lead-in to the listening. You'll notice that the teacher's manual provides an optional warm-up activity. That can be used either as the overall lesson warm-up or as an expansion activity sometime during the class, which serves to get the learners out of the book and interacting with each other.

The main listening tasks have the learners hear two people talking about their own schedule. The first time they listen, they order the pictures. The second time, they write times. Then they listen to five personalized questions about themselves *(What do you usually do for lunch? What do you like to do after school or work?)*.

The listening is at the beginning of the lesson. It serves to introduce the unit theme (schedules and routines) and grammar point (adverbs of frequency). The listening is followed up with major speaking activities including a pair work in which the students interview a partner and find similarities in how often they do things ranging from singing karaoke on weekends to eating too much. Following that, learners do a grammar and vocabulary review that allows them to consolidate their learning as they focus on form. Finally, there is a more open group work speaking activity where students discuss various topics, all of which are connected to personal activities.

This is typical of both listening lesson plans in particular and ESL lesson plans in general, in that it follows this pattern:

1. A warm-up activity
2. A meaning-based main listening task which (a) practices listening and (b) provides input and models for speaking tasks
3. A post-listening speaking activity. It is not uncommon for such an activity to have a high frequency use of target grammar, phrases,

and vocabulary. In that sense, it is drill-like, although certainly not limited to mechanical practice.

4. A language consolidation step. In traditional teaching, this was at the end of a lesson. We now understand that it is important to give students the opportunity to go back and focus on form to create the opportunity for acquisition, then to have the chance to continue using the language.

5. A more open fluency activity.

6. Assessing beginning learners

As Nunan (2004) points out, any teaching task is also potentially an assessment task. What separates a teaching task from an assessment task is that an assessment task should include a way to judge performance. For assessment, we need a way to get a score–though it doesn't need to be a numerical score at all. We simply have to be able to say how well the learners did and, perhaps but not always, how they compared to others. Another important difference between teaching and assessment tasks is that there should be a means to give feedback to students. We do this when we give grades, but feedback doesn't have to be a grade. Feedback can tell students their strengths and weaknesses, for example.

At the beginning level, learners are often asked **discrete test items**. Typical discrete items are about individual sounds (Did he say *ship* or *sheep*?), grammatical items, or words. In fact, the assumption seems to be that because they're beginning learners, they can only handle word-level (or below) understanding. Discrete item tests are often in a multiple-choice format. Students are asked to listen to a sentence and then choose one of two (or three or four…) alternatives. For example:

1. **a.** He did it.   2. **a.** He lives there.
   b. She did it.   **b.** He lived there.

These kinds of questions are not easy. They are also not especially useful as a real measurement of comprehension. The sentences look simple, but there is no context, so it is virtually impossible for even a native speaker of English to hear the differences between the sentences. When we listen in the real world, what we hear is part of a conversation, and we use the topic of the conversation (or our schema) to help us piece together what we don't understand.

Other ways that beginning level learners are often assessed are **cloze activities** and **dictation**. Cloze exercises ask the students to fill in the blanks in a text. Sometimes the text is a summary of what they have heard, sometimes individual sentences. Dictation is a familiar technique: the teacher reads sentences or a text and the learners write what they hear. Dictation has a long history in language teaching. Many people stopped using it for a time, but dictation may be a good test to show how learners integrate a number of skills. The most difficult thing about using dictation is the scoring of the tests. Generally, students should not be penalized for misspelling words (if you're testing listening, not spelling). They probably should get credit for writing a grammatical sentence that is similar to, but not exactly the same as, what was dictated. The key is fairness. The teacher needs to figure out the rules before grading the dictations. A similar technique is error correction, in which students listen to a text while looking at another that is very similar. They cross out (at a very beginning level) what is different from what they hear or (at a slightly higher level) they write the differences. All of these forms of assessment require students to work beyond the word level, integrating their understanding of the language. That's probably obvious in dictations, where they're writing complete sentences. But in cloze exercises and in error correction, they are using clues from the rest of the sentence as they fill in or correct individual word errors. Beginners should be assessed on their ability to use more than individual words.

Beginners can also be asked to choose the correct summary for a story or to say why the singer of a song was sad. They can be interviewed, asked simple questions. If the language they hear is at an appropriate level, and the assessment task is well made, longer listening texts are very good ways to assess beginners.

Assessment is not all about testing. Learners should have an opportunity throughout the class to be informally assessed. We'll talk about different ways to do this in other chapters, but one important aspect of informal assessment is giving credit for the listening done in class or as homework. Listening takes practice, and it makes sense to assess the practice rather than putting complete emphasis on tests. This might mean collecting examples of completed listening tasks, either individually or as part of a **portfolio** of work that is turned in at midterms and finals. A portfolio is simply a folder or envelope that contains a sample of a student's work. It may contain an introduction from the student explaining why the contents of the portfolio were chosen. Portfolios are useful because they give the teacher a look at student progress over the whole course and because they allow the students the opportunity to participate in building them. We'll discuss portfolios more later (page 122). Informal assessment could mean having the students use the self-study CDs that are often packaged in student books for homework, and collecting the homework. Actually, you don't have to "correct" the homework or the in-class listening tasks. It's enough to just give credit (a checkmark or circle for a complete assignment, a minus or x for an incomplete one) and add up all the assignments for a participation grade. One last example of informal assessment is observation. You'll want to move around the class as they listen to observe who is getting the answers quickly and who is struggling. Don't give grades (having you look over their shoulders will soon make people nervous), but be aware of what is going on while the listening tasks are being done.

7. Conclusion

In this chapter, we started out by defining some attributes of beginning level learners. We then stressed the importance of engaging beginning learners in many types of listening tasks and invited you, the reader, to consider what characteristics of tasks you find important. Comprehension happens at a variety of levels and our students need experience with them all. We have tried to share ways to support learners who find listening challenging. We have also laid the groundwork for looking at listening at an intermediate level, including looking at strategies for effective learning.

 **Further readings**

Day, R. and J. Park. 2005. Developing reading comprehension questions. *Reading in a Foreign Language,* 17 (1). Available online at: http://nflrc.hawaii.edu/rfl/April2005/day/day.html

Although the authors are discussing reading comprehension questions, they address many of the same issues we have addressed with levels of processing.

Lam, W.Y.K. 2002. Raising Students' Awareness of the Features of Real World Listening. In J.C. Richards and W.A. Renandya (eds.) *Methodology in Language Teaching: An Anthology of Current Practice.* Cambridge: Cambridge University Press. 248–253.

This text includes a useful discussion of the differences between spoken and written language.

Murphey, T. 1992. *Music and Song.* Oxford: Oxford University Press.

This "cookbook" styled collection of creative ways to use music in the classroom provides many useful and interesting ideas.

Nunan, D. and L. Miller. 1995. *New Ways in Teaching Listening.* Alexandria, VA: Teachers of English to Speakers of Other Languages.

Another "cookbook" with a wide range of tasks.

Helpful Web sites

These Web sites will be discussed more fully in Chapter 5. They both have a range of activities for listeners at all levels.

Arlyn Freed's ESL/EFL listening resources (www.eslhome.com/esl/listen/)

This site provides links for various Web sites that have on-line listening activities. The site also gives Ms. Freed's evaluations of the advantages and disadvantages of each site. The site is advertising free.

Randall's ESL Cyber Listening Lab (www.esl-lab.com/)

The listening lessons on this site all follow a three-step (pre-listening, listening, post-listening) format. The recordings are divded into easy, medium, and difficult levels. It is completely free.

References

American Council on the Teaching of Foreign Languages. 1986. ACTFL Proficiency Guidelines. Hasting-on-Hudson, NY: American Council on the Teaching of Foreign Languages.

Barrett, M.E. 1968. Cited in Alderson, C. and A. Uqart (eds.) *Reading in a foreign language.* 1984. Harlow, UK: Longman.

Bowen, T. and J. Marks. 1994. *Inside Teaching.* Oxford, UK: Macmillan Heinemann ELT.

Buck, G. 1995. "How to Become a Good Listening Teacher." In Mendelsohn, D. and J. Rubin (eds.) *A Guide for the Teaching of Second Language Listening.* San Diego, CA: Dominie Press.

Buck, G. 2001. *Assessing Listening.* Cambridge, UK: Cambridge University Press.

Cleary, C., B. Holden, and T. Cooney. 2003. *Top-Up Listening 1.* Tokyo, Japan: ABAX Ltd.

Dörnyei, Z. 2001. *Motivational Strategies in the Language Classroom.* Cambridge, UK: Cambridge University Press.

Flowerdew, J. and L. Miller. 2005. *Second Language Listening.* Cambridge, UK: Cambridge University Press.

Freeman, D., K. Graves, and L. Lee. 2005. *ICON Intro.* New York, NY: McGraw-Hill.

Helgesen, M., S. Brown, and T. Mandeville. 2004 *English Firsthand 1.* Hong Kong: Longman Asia ELT.

Helgesen, M., S. Brown, and T. Mandeville. 2004 *English Firsthand 1 Teacher's Manual.* Hong Kong: Longman Asia ELT.

Helgesen, M. and S. Brown. 1995. *Active Listening 1: Introducing Skills for Understanding.* Cambridge, UK: Cambridge University Press.

Howard, P. 2000 *The Owner's Manual for the Brain: Everyday Applications from Mind-Brain Research,* (2nd ed.) Atlanta, GA: Bard Press.

Nunan, D. 2003. *Listen In Book 1* (2nd ed.). Boston, MA: Heinle/Thomson.

Nunan, D. 2004. *Task-Based Language Teaching.* Cambridge, UK: Cambridge University Press.

Richards, J.C. and W. Renadya. 2002. *Methodology in Language Teaching: An anthology of current practice.* Cambridge, UK: Cambridge University Press.

Richards, J.C. 2003. *Developing Tactics in Listening* (2nd ed.). New York, NY: Oxford University Press.

Skehan, P. and P. Foster. 1997. "Task type and task processing conditions as influences on foreign language performance." *Language Teaching Research, 1, 3.* pp. 185–211.

Ur, P. 1984. *Teaching Listening Comprehension.* Cambridge, UK: Cambridge University Press.

Chapter **Three**

Listening for intermediate level learners

At the end of the chapter, you should be able to:

✔ **describe** characteristics of intermediate learners.

✔ **identify** variables that make a listening task easier or more challenging.

✔ **suggest** ways of helping learners deal with challenging listening tasks.

✔ **explain** language learning strategies.

✔ **give** examples of acquisition-friendly activities.

✔ **identify** self-assessment, communicative testing, and performance-based testing.

1. Introduction

In this chapter, we'll look at ways of teaching listening to intermediate level learners. Following the pattern established in Chapter 2, we begin by looking at syllabus design issues, in particular the question of difficulty. Next, we consider key concepts in working with intermediate students. We then look at the listening classroom and how the syllabus design issues and key concepts come into play as we teach. Finally, we look at assessment issues that can arise when testing listening skills.

Reflection

Before we begin, it is useful to think about the learners we are talking about. It is fairly easy to define what a beginning or an advanced level learner is. However, because it is in the middle of the scale, "intermediate" is a more challenging term to categorize.

Based on your experience as a language learner, non-native speakers of your language you have met, and any other experiences you have, answer these questions.

1. What things can intermediate students do? What things do they find difficult?

2. How would you define an intermediate level learner?

3. When they are in a situation where they don't understand the speaker, what do intermediate learners do to try to help themselves understand, either by trying to change the way the speaker is talking or by doing something to bolster their own comprehension?

Share your answers with a classmate or colleague.

What is intermediate listening ability? The ACTFL proficiency ratings for listening say that a person at the intermediate level of proficiency should be able to understand:

- content referring to personal background and needs.
- sentences that are a combination of phrases that the learner has already learned.
- everyday situations, for example travel: lodging, transportation, shopping.
- short telephone conversations, simple announcements, and some news reports.

- Intermediate students still have trouble when the conversation changes time or direction.
- Understanding may be uneven and incomplete.

2. Syllabus design issues

It's not how difficult the listening is. It is how the listening is difficult.

When anyone, student or teacher, runs into difficulty while listening in a foreign or second language, it is easy to say, "That is just too difficult."

Think of a time you had difficulty understanding something you heard. It could be when you were trying to listen to another language, or it could be a time you heard something in your own language that was difficult to understand because of level (a very academic lecture on an unknown subject), dialect (e.g., some speakers of North American English have difficulty with Scottish or New Zealand English), content and culture (the lyrics of a song from a culture you don't know much about—Country and Western or Hip-hop are examples for some people), or any other reason.

Why was it difficult? Write nine things you think made the listening difficult.

- _____
- _____
- _____
- _____
- _____
- _____
- _____
- _____
- _____

Share your list with a classmate or colleague.

How easy or difficult listening is depends on the text, the task, the speaker, and the listener. Of course, all these factors interact with each other, but for the sake of clarity we will use these four categories. (This is our version of ideas that have been presented by Anderson and Lynch 1988, Buck 2001, and Nunan 2004.)

The Text

- **Parts of language.** Learners may have difficulties with speech rate (too fast or slow); pausing (too much or too little); unfamiliar words; unfamiliar pronunciation of known words; unfamiliar intonation of sentences; unfamiliar grammatical structures.

- **Usage of language**. Learners may have difficulties because of a lack of familiarity with the way language is used. They may have problems with **functional language** like apologizing or requesting. They may also lack familiarity with conventions of direct and indirect speech (hinting, joking, etc.).
- **Amount of language**. Learners may have difficulties because there is too little or too much information in the text. **Redundancy** (saying the same thing again, either simply repeating or using different words) may make listening easier. It may make listening more difficult if the listener thinks it's just more to hear.
- **Organization**. Learners may have difficulties if the text is organized in unfamiliar ways or uses flashbacks, extra comments not related to the main idea, etc.
- **Content**. Learners will have an easier time with familiar topics and familiar vocabulary.
- **Amount of context**. Learners will have an easier time understanding if they know what has come before the text they are listening to, what the relationship of the speakers is, etc.
- **Kind of text**. Learners will understand stories more easily than debates, for example.

The Task

- **Complexity of the task**. Fewer demands on learner knowledge and memory make tasks easier. Breaking the task into steps helps understanding. Having information in one place (not spread out all over the page, for example) helps. Not presenting too much information will make the task easier.
- **Level of response required**. Checking a box may be (but not necessarily always is) easier than writing a word. Giving a summary is more difficult than giving details.
- **Level of participation**. Sometimes, it may be easier to be overhearing than talking to another person. At other times, the context of having a conversational partner makes things easier to understand.
- **Knowledge of the content and procedure of the task**. Topics that learners know about are easier to work with. Tasks that have been done before are easier to do the second time.
- **Level of support/context**. Pictures, or having the task presented in helpful ways (graphically), may make understanding easier.
- **Response time**. How much time is given and how long it has been since learners listened will have an effect on completion of the task. This is why comprehension questions may be more difficult than they seem. They typically come after the listening is finished, and so they're a kind of memory test.

The Speaker

Many of the categories for the text overlap with categories for the speaker, since the speaker is speaking the text. Other factors are:

- **Style**. The speaker may have an individual style of speaking that is difficult to understand.
- **Accent**. The speaker may have an unfamiliar accent.
- **Number of speakers**. Listening to one person is usually easier than listening to many people.
- **Recorded or not**. Whether the speaker is recorded or is a live conversation partner can make a difference in understanding.

The Listener

- **Proficiency level**. Advanced learners understand more than beginning learners.
- **Interest and motivation**. It's hard to listen to something that you're not really interested in. Learner motivation plays a big part in all language learning.
- **Confidence**. Sometimes a lack of success in previous classes makes learners give up. It's hard to listen effectively when you have no confidence.

Anderson and Lynch (1988) used the analogy of slide controls (equalizers) in a recording studio. See Figure 1. As teachers, we can raise and lower the level on each characteristic to match our learners' levels. We can update that metaphor by thinking about the various controls on a computer. Raising items to the top makes them more challenging. Lowering them to the bottom makes them easier.

Task:

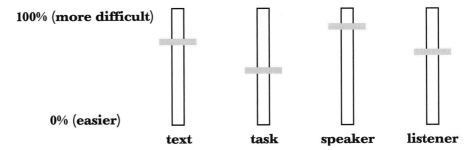

Figure 1: Controlling factors of a listening task

Think of any listening task. The easiest way is to choose one from the CD from this book. However, it could also be one you've taught or experienced in a language class, or one you've experienced in a real life situation.

Use the "computer slide control" metaphor. How could you raise or lower the variables in the task? Try to think of at least two actions for each. If you are using this book in a class, you may want to do this step with a partner, seeing how many different possibilities you can come up with. Afterwards, compare your ideas with another pair of students.

The ideas you come up with will, of course, depend on the task, the students, and many other things. Here are a few ideas:

The Text

- Preteach key vocabulary.
- Modify the script to make the language level easier or harder. If that isn't practical, try one of the following.
- Give a short talk before the recording that previews the content (activate schema).
- Follow up the recording with a talk that gives additional information.
- For non-fiction topics, put the learners into small groups and have them see how much they already know about the topic.

The Task

- Write a list of key words on the board to help guide them.
- Add pictures. For example, find related pictures on the Internet and have students preview by talking about what they think they will hear.
- Modify the task to include TPR (see page 44), drawing, etc.
- Provide a copy of the script for students to use at some time during the activity (not the whole time).

The Speaker

- Have more or fewer speakers. You can do this if you are making your own material, but it is probably not practical if you are using a textbook. In that case, try one of these other ideas.
- Pause the recording to allow "think time."
- Read the script yourself, rather than using the recording (at least the first time).
- Play the recording a second or third time.

The Listener

- Give the learners a choice of two to three ways to respond (e.g., draw a picture, write the key words, write a summary).
- Have the learners do the task in pairs, sharing what they understand.
- Add a microtask like those described in Chapter 2, pp. 36–37.

3. Principles for teaching listening to intermediate learners

1. Teach listening strategies.

There's a website called Dave Sperling's ESL Cafe (www.eslcafe.com). We went there and, in the student discussion area, posted this message:

Dave Sperling presents the One and Only

Dave's ESL Cafe

The Internet's Meeting place for ESL + EFL teachers + students from around the World!

Posted by Marcos on Monday, 1 February, at 6:55 p.m.

- What do you do to improve your listening? Movies and TV are too difficult for me.

These are the responses I got the next day:

- Hi Marcos.
  I think that you should grab some movie scripts (there are plenty of them on the web) and then try to watch movies with "a little help" from them.
  Jarek.

- You can listen to English songs and listen to radio programs.
  Mohamed

- First, you can purchase a tape-recorder/cheap one/. Every library has a plenty of tapes for practice. Also listening video-tapes with your famous films can help. You can see it and listen few times if you don't understand at first. Otherwise, listening radio and TV news is realy the best of all. Or! listen people conversation on the street, in the bus or train! It's not polite, but can help a lot!!!
  Good luck! Vesna.

(continued)

> • Marcos,
> There are many ways to learn English in a non-speaking environment. To begin with you should locate the nearest bookstore that stocks up english books. Next, select books that are simple to read. Slowly progress to more difficult books when you gain sufficient confidence. Xin Xin, a classmate of mine has suggested that you buy English conversational tapes to practise speaking the language. Karen, on the other hand, believes that listening to English news is vital to the learning of the language. However, I hope you have cabled television. CNN and BBC are great news channels. Aisyah thinks having a pen-pal who writes to you in English allows you to use the language effectively. If all these fail, Shihui firmly believes arming yourself with a bilingual dictionary will see you through many storms.:)(suppose to be smiley).
> Lots of love and luck from 202 of RGS (Singapore)

What all of these people are talking about are **learning strategies**—learners taking conscious steps to work on language and to be aware of how they learn. Basically, anything you do to learn or to be aware of your learning constitutes a strategy.

Reflection

1. If you have studied a foreign or second language, what things do (or did) you do other than take classes to help you learn? Did you do things to work on listening in particular?

2. Were they effective? Why or why not?

3. What can people in your country, who are learning the language, do outside of class to become better listeners?

Share your answers with a classmate or colleague.

While learning strategies can be and are used at all levels of language learning, for many students, the intermediate level is the time when they really begin to take control of their own learning and identify those ways of learning they like best.

There are a number of systems for categorizing learning strategies. Indeed, one of the frustrating things about learning strategies is that there are so many systems and lists of language learning strategies that the numbers can be mind-boggling. One excellent book (Flowerdew and Miller, 2005) identified 34 strategies used specifically for listening. An earlier classic on language learning strategies (Oxford, 1990) listed nearly 90.

While all the strategies can be useful, we find it helpful to teach students a smaller number of listening strategies that they can remember and practice often enough to apply. Rost (2002) has identified six strategies successful second language listeners use.

Read the list of Rost's listening strategies of successful second language learners. Then write specific things you could do to teach/practice each one.

1. **Predicting** – Successful learners predict information before listening.

   Your idea: _I could have my students..._ _____

   _____

2. **Inferencing** – Successful learners draw inferences (listen between the lines) when information is incomplete. (As we mentioned earlier, building in inference can be tricky since it depends so much on the text. Thinking about emotions and whether the topic discussed is new or not new is one way.)

   Your idea: _____

   _____

3. **Monitoring** – Successful learners notice what they are and are not understanding as they listen.

   Your idea: _____

   _____

4. **Clarifying** – Successful learners ask questions when they don't understand.

   Your idea: _____

   _____

5. **Responding** – Successful learners provide "a personal, relevant response to the information ideas presented," (i.e., they interact).

   Your idea: _____

   _____

6. Evaluating – Successful learners check on how well they understood. Were they able to complete the task? (This is done at the end of the task, whereas number 3 is during listening.)

Your idea: _____

_____

How many of these have you tried when learning a language?

Share your answers with a classmate or colleague.

In Section 4, we'll look at ways a number of these listening strategies are approached in textbooks.

2. Balance "listening as comprehension practice" and "listening for acquisition."

Most of what we have suggested so far in this book is listening as comprehension. That is, we have been looking at ways to help learners understand the meaning of what they hear. That is clearly their most important, immediate goal.

However, in the past few years, researchers have become increasingly certain that taking the time to notice language forms, pieces of grammar, new words, etc., can make it easier to acquire those forms. When we think of **acquisition**, we don't mean "learning" in the sense of studying and remembering, like much of what learners do at school. We mean the unconscious ability to understand and use language—much the way we all acquired our first language.

Richards (2005) argues that "consciousness of features of ... input can serve as a trigger which activates the first stage in the process of incorporating new linguistic features into one's language competence."

Although that might sound complicated, it is actually quite simple. If you've ever had the chance to learn a language in an environment where the language is used, you've probably experienced it. You find out about some feature of the language—a new bit of grammar or perhaps a new word. You think, "Really, I've never heard that." Then you go out into "the real world" and realize you are hearing it all the time. You had just never noticed.

Meaning has to come first. If you listen to something without understanding, you're not learning anything. Once learners have understood the meaning, they can move on to **Focus on Form (FonF)** activities that allow them to notice the way things are being said. The process is something like this:

1. First you understand the meaning.
2. Then you notice the form.

3. Once you notice the form, you can start to notice the gap between the way you are using that structure and the actual target form.

4. Once you notice that gap, you can start to close the gap.

This changes the input we've received from listening into conscious **intake**. We might think of this as acquisition-friendly listening. Again, this is something we should do at all levels, but at the intermediate level, learners have enough language to effectively discuss their learning in ways that are useful in these form-focused contexts. In the next section, "Tasks and materials," we'll show you examples of how this can be done in listening activities.

Reflection

1. Have you had an experience in language learning when having a form brought to consciousness made it more noticeable? When did it happen? How did it affect your recognizing the form in listening? In speaking?

2. Can you think of ways you can encourage your students to notice form during listening tasks?

Share your answers with a classmate or colleague.

Richards (2005, p. 90) identifies several ways to help students "notice." They can listen again to a recording in order to:

- identify differences between what they hear and a printed version of the text.
- complete a cloze version of the text.
- complete sentence stems taken from a text.
- check off, from a list, expressions that occurred in the text.

Richards also suggests it is important to move beyond receptive understanding to "restructuring" activities that let students apply what they have noticed to their spoken language. Pair readings of scripts and role plays are possible ways to do this.

Action

1. Think of a listening task. Again, it could be one from this book or one you've taught or experienced in a language class.

2. Assume that you are teaching it in class. Once learners have finished the meaning-based main task, what could you have them do to notice the key language (examples of main grammar points, functional phrases, etc.)? What could you do to help them move from noticing to restructuring—using the target forms on their own?

3. See how many different ideas you can come up with.

If possible, you may want to do this as a brainstorm with classmates or colleagues.

---

3. Go a little further.

You probably noticed that the ACTFL definitions at the beginning of this chapter indicated that what separates intermediate learners from beginning learners is not their ability to deal with meaning and form, but their ability to deal with longer, more complete texts. It is very useful to look for ways to encourage students not only to deal with longer texts for listening, but also to push themselves beyond the specific task on a textbook page to notice extra information and think about how they arrived at the answers they did.

This process may also involve moving beyond the specific listening task and using the information heard in a speaking, reading, or writing task. Restructuring tasks in which learners role play the next scene or write their ideas about what they heard are simple examples of this.

4. Tasks and materials

In the previous section, we stressed the importance of strategies, of balancing tasks for comprehension and those for acquisition, and of encouraging learners to "go further." In this section, we'll look at ways those ideas can become part of classroom practice, both as they appear in textbooks and as things teachers can do to add them if they are using books which lack these elements. As mentioned earlier, these strategies can take place at any level of learning. However, intermediate students are often more aware of their learning so this seems a good time to move beyond "catching the answers" to more consciousness of how we try to make sense of what we hear. In this section, we will describe the following strategies and illustrate how to use them with classroom tasks:

1. Predicting
2. Inferencing
3. Monitoring
4. Clarifying
5. Responding
6. Evaluation

1. Predicting

The first strategy is **predicting**. Predicting serves many functions including **schema** activation and **task awareness**. In Chapter 2, we stressed the usefulness of pre-listening tasks that activate previously known words and content (schema). When learners are predicting, it means they have to look over the task so they are automatically engaging in this schema activation. Prediction also ensures that learners think about the task they will attempt; thus, raising their task awareness. Finally, just the act of predicting can often increase the learners' interest. They've made a guess and want to find out whether or not they were right.

Example 1

CD Track 12

Sound Bytes 2 (Gershon and Mares, 2000, p.115)

Example 1 on page 71 shows a preview activity of a comprehension task. The students will hear a fairly long segment about job interviews. Before they listen, they look over a series of suggestions. They circle the ones they think will be included. Then they listen and check the ones they actually do hear.

Action

1. Before listening to the extract for Example 1, actually try a prediction activity. Read the items in the "Job interview—Before the interview" box. Circle the items you think will be included in the talk.

2. Now listen to Track 12 on the CD for this book or read the extract in Appendix 2 (page 165). Check the items you do hear.

Many books don't include prediction as a pre-listening task. You can, however, often add it yourself. Just have the learners look over the listening lesson and ask them to give the answers they think would be correct, ways they would answer if they were being asked the questions that are likely to be asked of the people in the recording, or even–based on what is written–guess the questions they think might be asked.

Prediction can also take place at the word level. In Chapter 2, we mentioned that in cloze activities, we can ask learners to fill in the blanks before they listen.

Example 2

CD Track 13

> **1** Sunny wrote a letter to her university's student newspaper. Fill in the spaces. There is one extra word.
>
> | campus | discrimination | attention | harassment |
> | improve | comments | ~~nationality~~ | reasons |
>
> Dear Editor,
> Discrimination is wrong. These days, everyone agrees that people who dislike other people because of their skin color or _nationality_ are foolish racists. But what about sexual discrimination and sexual _____? On _____, it takes many forms. Some professors pay more attention to male students than to women. The men, they say, will become political and business leaders. Others pay _____ to the women but for the wrong _____. We don't want _____ about our fashion and our bodies. We are in school to _____ our minds. And, when we go to parties with male students, we want respect. No unwanted touching. Treat us like we are your equals. We are!
> Sunny Wu

Now listen and check your answers.

English Firsthand 2 (Helgesen, Brown, and Mandeville, 2004, p. 105)

Notice the instructions in Example 2. Step 1 asks the learners to fill in the spaces. They don't listen to the listening passage until after they have completed the cloze activity. This, of course, is primarily a reading activity that uses listening as the checking phase. It comes at the end of a unit in which students were practicing stating opinions. This type of activity fits in to the listening for acquisition task that Richards (2005) advocates, in that it asks learners not only to do a cloze activity but later also asks learners to do a type of role play in which they write about something at school or in their city, then read and discuss it with a partner. Of course, this also encourages learners to keep going and not stop with finding the correct answers.

It is even possible and useful to predict at the level of sounds. Look at the pronunciation activity in Example 3 (page 74). The learner is asked to predict where an extra sound is inserted in some sentences.

Example 3

CD Track 14

5

A In spoken English, a /w/ sound is sometimes inserted between words in a process known as intrusion. Listen to the example.

> **Example:** I never do any e-mailing. (no intrusion)
> I never do$_w$any e-mailing. (/w/ intrusion)

B Look at these sentences and predict where you might hear a /w/ intrusion. Now listen and check.

1. I have no online access from this computer.
2. Helen isn't an Internet addict, but you are!
3. Even though I was really tired, I had to go on.
4. Go under the bridge, then go through another tunnel.
5. You and I are going to an event tonight.
6. I have to do another two exercises before I can finish.

C Listen again. Practice with a partner. Can you think of any rules for when /w/ intrusion might take place?

Listen In Book 3 (Nunan, 2003, p. 66)

Reflection

Before you listen to Example 3, try the task in Step B. As you do, notice that to do the task, you have to say each sentence (aloud or mentally), and you have to listen to yourself to find the correct location.

Then listen to Track 14 or check the script in Appendix 2 (page 166) to be sure.

Action

1. Flip through this book. Stop at any textbook page example. Imagine that you are teaching that lesson. What could you do to have students predict?

2. Do this three or four times. Can you find different ways of predicting?

Share your answers with a classmate or colleague.

2. Inferencing

The next strategy is making **inferences**. Students are sometimes unaware of how often English speakers—native as well as non-native—speak indirectly. And while directly stated information is essential, it is often fairly easy to understand. Unstated or implied information can be a challenge.

Example 4

CD Track 15

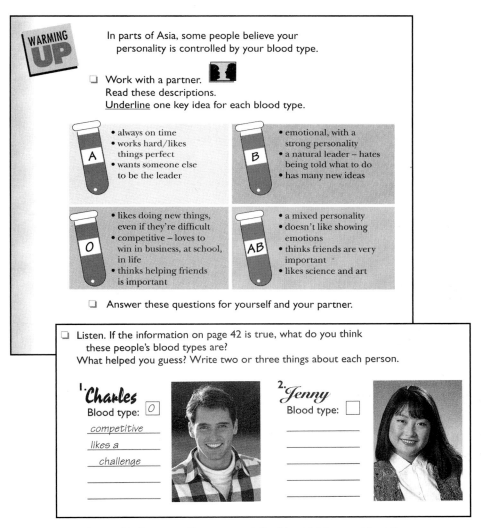

Active Listening 3 (Helgesen, Brown, and Smith, 1996, pp. 42–43)

Example 4 (page 75) shows an activity specifically designed for practicing inferences. The students are hearing information about personality and blood types. In the warm-up, they have read about blood types and thought about their own personalities. As you listen to Example 4, notice that the speaker never says what her blood type is. The listener is, however, able to infer the answer.

Inference is not limited to those activities that are designed to teach and practice it. Example 5 below was not designed as an inference task. The tasks on the page include prediction, gist (main ideas), and responding.

Audio

Example 5

CD Track 16

Real World Listening

Unit **17**

1 *Predict*
A man is talking to someone about his late wife.
What do you think he will talk about?

☐ how they first met ☐ how lonely he is
☐ her last few days ☐ their children
☐ good times they had together ☐ another topic?

🎧 Now listen and check your prediction.

2 *Get the main ideas*
How does Mr. Hayes respond to these things that the host says?

1. *Do you mind telling us how she died?*
   ☐ **a.** She died in her sleep. It was very sudden.
   ☐ **b.** Cancer. She had it for about a year.
2. *You get to know someone pretty well in 56 years, don't you?*
   ☐ **a.** When they're gone, there's a big hole that no one can fill up.
   ☐ **b.** Actually, you think you get to know them, but you really don't.
3. *I imagine you have some wonderful memories, as well.*
   ☐ **a.** We had a lot of good times, Maggie and me.
   ☐ **b.** I really don't feel like talking about it anymore.

3 *Respond to the ideas*
1. Mr. Hayes says, "You share so many years of your life with someone, and when they're gone, there's a big hole that no one can fill up." How do you think he could try to fill that hole? What could he do to ease his loneliness?
2. What could you do to help someone deal with the loss of a family member?

Impact Listening 3 (Harsch and Wolfe-Quintero, 2001, p. 41)

Listen to Example 5. What do you feel you know about the man that he does not say specifically? Write four things.

- _____   • _____

- _____   • _____

Share your answers with a classmate or colleague.

When answering the question in the Action box above, many people identify things like *He loved her very much. He is still in love with her. He misses her.* You might also assume that the interviewee is a fairly quiet, unassuming man. He doesn't say those things directly, but we can assume them from what he does say and the way he says it. Activities like this—where we are thinking deeply about what we hear—make the text more real in our minds and encourage us to think more deeply. Just adding this type of "listening for inference" task to a textbook activity is a way to help learners practice this deeper-level understanding skill.

Notice that the activity in Example 5 works nicely with the suggestions for moving from comprehension to acquisition-friendly listening. The listener identifies Clayton's responses, then follows it up with personalized responses. In the actual book, the learners also have a self-study page where they listen as they read the script with 20 two-to-six-word phrases missing. They match those phrases, which appear at the top of the page, to the correct locations.

3. Monitoring

The next strategy is **monitoring**. It is important for learners to pay attention to what they are understanding and what they are missing. This strategy is rare in textbooks, except in the sense that teachers often check answers after a task. While this is useful and necessary, it is also "after the fact." It focuses on product—what was understood—rather than process: how the understanding takes place. Example 6 (page 78) includes ideas from a teacher's manual that encourage monitoring.

Example 6

> *Options and variations*
>
> ◆ **Extra preparation: Listening warm-up**
> Write the following words on the board in a list: *like to, how about, sorry, wait, do you want, really sorry, I haven't, too bad, why don't you, maybe, I didn't, why, Do you plan.*
> Students close their books. They listen one time. Each time they hear one of the words or phrases, they raise their hands. By raising their hands, they help alert other students who missed or were unsure about what they heard.

> *Options and variations*
>
> ◆ **Extra preparation**
> On the board, write *How would you change if you lived in another country for more than one year?* Have the learners discuss this in their first language. Encourage them to include ideas and examples if they know people who have done this. Then, ask them to try to have the same conversation in English. They say the same things, but this time try to do it in English.
> ♣ You may want to have students compare answers in pairs before checking. This allows students to sort through the information and decide which items to write. Also, since some of the ideas may be new to them, it allows them to share information and understanding with each other.

English Firsthand 2 Teacher's Manual

(Helgesen, Brown, and Mandeville, 2004, pp. T45 and T53).

Example 7

CD Track 17

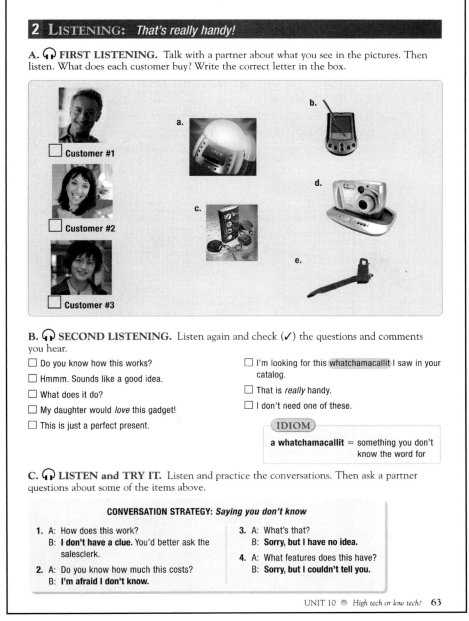

2 LISTENING: *That's really handy!*

A. 🎧 FIRST LISTENING. Talk with a partner about what you see in the pictures. Then listen. What does each customer buy? Write the correct letter in the box.

Customer #1

Customer #2

Customer #3

a.

b.

c.

d.

e.

B. 🎧 SECOND LISTENING. Listen again and check (✓) the questions and comments you hear.

☐ Do you know how this works?

☐ Hmmm. Sounds like a good idea.

☐ What does it do?

☐ My daughter would *love* this gadget!

☐ This is just a perfect present.

☐ I'm looking for this whatchamacallit I saw in your catalog.

☐ That is *really* handy.

☐ I don't need one of these.

> **IDIOM**
>
> **a whatchamacallit** = something you don't know the word for

C. 🎧 LISTEN and TRY IT. Listen and practice the conversations. Then ask a partner questions about some of the items above.

CONVERSATION STRATEGY: *Saying you don't know*

1. A: How does this work?
B: **I don't have a clue.** You'd better ask the salesclerk.

2. A: Do you know how much this costs?
B: **I'm afraid I don't know.**

3. A: What's that?
B: **Sorry, but I have no idea.**

4. A: What features does this have?
B: **Sorry, but I couldn't tell you.**

UNIT 10 ⊛ *High tech or low tech?* 63

ICON 2 (Freeman, Graves, and Lee, 2005, p. 63)

4. Clarifying

The next strategy is **clarifying**. Example 7 on page 79 provides a good example of this. The learners see pictures of five electronic products that they are unlikely to recognize. Notice that they are taught the idiom "watchamacallit" for an unknown word. They are also given the word in a sentence, *I'm looking for this whatchamacallit I saw in your catalog.* First they listen and identify the item. Then they listen again to note the questions and comments they hear.

Of course, the second listening task works toward listening for acquisition because it helps learners notice the forms they need. The third step, "Listen and try it," moves the learners into restructuring by having learners practice the "Saying you don't know" mini-conversations—dialogue practice—and then asking and answering their own questions.

Example 8

Beating around the Bush (Maley, in *Top Class Activities 2,* 2000, P. Watcyn-Jones (ed.) p. 73)

Maley (2000) provides the listening/speaking activity shown in Example 8. The learners are given pictures of items they are unlikely to know how to say in English. They are also given explaining phrases like *You use it for ...-ing., It's made of... and, it's about the size of....* They give their hints about objects. Partners listen and try to figure out what is being described.

5. Responding

A good way to have learners practice the strategy of **responding** with personal, relevant information is to have the recording of the listening directed at the learners themselves. In Example 9, the learners listen to partial sentences about their own superstitions and beliefs. They complete the sentences with their own ideas. This not only provides practice in the responding strategy, it meets one of the suggestions for acquisition-friendly listening practice.

Example 9

Active Listening 3 (Helgesen, Brown, and Smith 1996, p. 26)

Murphey (2001) advocates "interactional shadowing" during listening as a way of focusing the learner's attention and encouraging responding. A student can repeat the key words or the last words a speaker says to confirm understanding. See Example 10.

Example 10

Language Hungry (Murphey, 1998, p. 14)

6. Evaluation

The final strategy is **evaluation**. Students need to reflect on what they did and didn't understand. This may be as simple as giving a few minutes of quiet time at the end of a lesson to think about what the learners did and didn't understand.

Evaluation will be discussed more fully in the section of this chapter on assessment, but before leaving this section we'd like to share a simple, generic form we use in our own classes. It includes listening as well as other skills. It can be used at the end of a particular class or once every few weeks, in which case the learners reflect on the course generally. We find it gives us the information we need to modify future lesson plans. It also helps the students think about their own learning and success.

Class _____

Feed~~back~~ Forward

Please rate the things we do in this class.

☺	☺	☺
5= very	3 = so-so	1 = not at all

	Useful	Interesting	Easy (Level of "challenge" was good)	How much did you try?
Listening	_____	_____	_____	_____
Conversation	_____	_____	_____	_____
Pair work/ Group work	_____	_____	_____	_____
Homework	_____	_____	_____	_____
Activities not from the book	_____	_____	_____	_____
Trying to use English in class	_____	_____	_____	_____
Trying to use English outside of class	_____	_____	_____	_____

During speaking activities, how much English do you usually use? _____%

PELT Listening (Helgesen & Brown) © McGraw-Hill. Permission granted to copy for classroom use.

Throughout this chapter, we have looked at ways to use the "good listener" strategies and have mentioned ways that tasks can help ensure understanding and facilitate acquisition. We have also mentioned helping students go further, sometimes by using what they heard as the basis for an activity such as a role play or question/answer task. The last example (Example 11) shows a very simple way to encourage learners to go further: play the recording again and ask them to catch extra information.

Example 11

CD Track 18

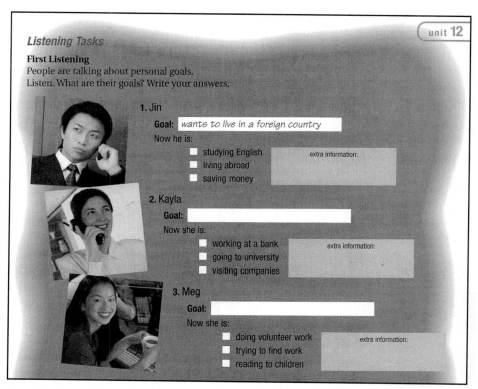

Listening Tasks   unit 12

First Listening
People are talking about personal goals.
Listen. What are their goals? Write your answers.

1. Jin
Goal: *wants to live in a foreign country*
Now he is:
- [ ] studying English
- [ ] living abroad
- [ ] saving money

extra information:

2. Kayla
Goal:
Now she is:
- [ ] working at a bank
- [ ] going to university
- [ ] visiting companies

extra information:

3. Meg
Goal:
Now she is:
- [ ] doing volunteer work
- [ ] trying to find work
- [ ] reading to children

extra information:

English Firsthand 2 (Helgesen, Brown, and Mandeville, 2004, p. 107)

Reflection

Which of the tasks that you listened to (or read) stand out the most in your mind? Why?

Share your answer with a classmate or colleague.

5. Listening in the intermediate classroom

In Chapters 1 and 2, we pointed out that most listening lessons have three parts:

- a pre-listening warm-up
- the listening task
- a post-listening task which often involves speaking or other productive skills

But, of course, classroom listening practice doesn't happen in a vacuum. Usually time is required for the other skills of speaking, reading, and writing and for other language work such as vocabulary, grammar, pronunciation, strategy training, etc. And very often those other skills and aspects of language are taught by the teacher at least in part orally, so the students need to listen to understand.

All of this brings up the question of the location of listening in a lesson plan and the making of that plan itself. Some courses, especially those at university **Intensive English Programs (IEPs)**, specify the purpose of various classes according to skills. There may be a separate listening class. In that case, the "three point plan" listed above will often be the way you want to structure a lesson. And, of course, when possible, it is useful for there to be at least an awareness and perhaps real coordination between what is taught in the listening course and what happens in the other classes.

Often, however, listening is one component of a listening/speaking course or of a four-skills (listening/speaking/reading/writing) course. In that case, you need to think about where in the lesson you want to put the listening part of the lesson.

Action

Imagine you are teaching a listening-speaking or a four-skills course. Assume the class meets for one hour or ninety minutes. Why might you teach listening at the beginning of the class? In the middle? Toward the end?

Write a few reasons for each placement.

Beginning	Middle	End

Share your ideas with a classmate or colleague.

Reasons to teach listening at the beginning of class

The most obvious reason, perhaps, is **input**. We know that for learning and acquisition to take place, students need to meet new language. If we look at this as happening at the beginning of a learning cycle, in this case a class, and we believe listening can be a useful way of providing input, this can be a strong rationale for putting listening at the beginning.

Also, since listening is receptive, it means learners can practice this skill early in the class, before they are able to produce the language themselves. The way you understand the process of language teaching/learning/acquisition may also influence your decision. For many years **Presentation → Practice → Production (P-P-P)** was the most common model for language teaching. Simply put, the model said learners should first be presented with the language they will be expected to produce. Listening can be a very good way to do this presentation. That stage is followed by controlled practice activities such as drills, dialogues, pair work, and games that have a great deal of practice of the target forms. This is followed by the production stage which allows more open language use.

There are many reasons that P-P-P is not considered a particularly accurate model. It treats language is if it were linear—things are learned in a straight line. First you master *language point a*, then go on to master *point b*, then *c*, etc. Language learning is much more complex than that. Students are all at different levels of mastery on different language points. And some are just acquired later than others. However, despite problems with the P-P-P model, it remains popular in many places around the world, perhaps because it is seen as very teachable.

In a P-P-P class, listening usually goes at the beginning. Of course, putting it at the beginning doesn't alone make a class P-P-P. Every model of language learning demands input and that input might well come at the beginning.

Putting listening in the middle of the lesson

If we believe listening is useful for input, sometimes we want to create a need for that input. For example, doing a speaking activity at the beginning of class can help learners realize the information they need to do a given listening task correctly and can be a way to provide focus. In that case, you may want to put the listening in the middle of the lesson.

A more recent model of language learning is **Task-based Learning (TBL)**, which Richards and Schmidt (2002) define as an approach "based on the use of communicative and interactive tasks as the central units for the planning and delivery of instruction" (p. 540). One form of TBL can be referred to as "fluency first" because learners go immediately into communication tasks, then move toward activities that let them **Focus on Form** and do accuracy-based work. From there, they go back to fluency work which is, hopefully, influenced by what they have noticed in their accuracy work. The acquisition-friendly activities in the "Tasks and materials" section of this chapter (page 70) are examples of listening tasks that could be used in this way.

Listening at the end of class

This is probably the least common location for listening, but there are reasons you might want to try it. It can be a way for learners to review what they did, either in the class that is just finished or in previous classes. And a few minutes of listening review with time to reflect on what they are learning can let learners mentally recycle the new vocabulary, forms, and content they have learned.

One way of using listening (and any other task) at the end of class is *task recycling*. Lynch and Maclean (2001) suggest that giving learners a chance to repeat activities leads to real learning and progress. Some teachers are hesitant to repeat activities. Our own experience suggests, however, that learners often appreciate the opportunity to review.

Lesson planning

Questions about where to place listening in your lesson bring us to the important issue of lesson planning.

Reflection

Think about these questions concerning lesson plans. If you are not yet teaching, think about your future classroom and what you might do.

1. When you are teaching, do you write out your lesson plan? If so, in what style (goals and objectives, full notes, brief notes, etc.)?

2. How long in advance do you plan? One class? One week? One month? A full course?

3. Does having a written lesson plan make it easier or more difficult to do spontaneous things/take advantage of opportunities in class?

Share your answers with a colleague or classmate.

We recall a graduate school class on listening methodology a few years ago. The question of lesson planning came up. Students were talking about their various styles of planning, the problems with their schools' curricula, etc., when one student said, "Lesson plans are nonsense. They are just something we had to do during practice teaching. Nobody really writes out long lesson plans." A lively debate followed. At one point, a student paused. She had a look like a light bulb had just lit up in her head. She said, "I just thought of something. We always have a lesson plan. If I write it myself, I decide what I'm going to do. If I don't, I have to follow the textbook, so that means I have to use the author's lesson plan. And the author doesn't know me, my students, my teaching style. Writing plans gives me control."

We agree with our grad student. Your own lesson plans put you in control. And they are likely to be more satisfying to you and your students because they are designed to meet the needs of the class.

Farrell (2002) identifies four important benefits of lesson planning:

- "A plan can help the teacher think about content, materials, sequencing, timing and activities.
- A plan provides security (in the form of a map) in the sometimes unpredictable atmosphere of a classroom.
- A plan can be a log of what has been taught.
- A plan can help a substitute to smoothly take over a class when the teacher cannot teach."

Of course, you are not completely on your own in making your plan. In Chapter 2, we pointed out that many teacher's manuals provide a great deal of support. Other books and websites such as those that provide expansion activities and the ideas in books like this one can help, too.

How do you make a lesson plan?

There are many ways to get started. We often recommend that beginning teachers start by using their textbook's teacher's manual. At some point, you'll start thinking *I know that.* Or *I can do it better a different way.* Wonderful. That means you probably want to start writing your own plans.

Here are some things to think about:

- What are the goals? What do I want learners to accomplish by the end of class?
- What listening activities will they do?
- How will I include a pre-listening warm-up?
- How will I follow up the listening task(s)?
- Will I be including an acquisition/FonF task as well as a meaning-based task?
- What other skills will I include in the lesson?
- What am I doing to get the student interested in and involved with the tasks?
- What sequence will I teach the activities in? (Notice the balance of long/short, exciting/less exciting, input/production tasks, etc.)
- How long will each activity take?

Harmer (1998) offers good advice when he suggests that any successful lesson plan needs to do three things: engage the students, help them study, and activate students' knowledge.

What form should a lesson plan take?

The graduate student who complained that no one really writes out long lesson plans had a point. When he was first training to be a teacher, he was required to do long lesson plans. They may be useful for helping new teachers really think through their goals and plans but, day to day, most teachers write in a personal shorthand. Codes like $T \rightarrow Ss$ (Teachers to the students) or $S \leftarrow \rightarrow S$ (students interacting with each other) are very common.

Basically, your lesson plan can take any form that (a) helps you think through the class before you teach it and (b) helps you while you are teaching the lesson.

Action

Choose a listening task from this book or elsewhere.

1. Look at the list of "things to think about" on page 88.

2. Decide where in an overall English lesson you would put listening (beginning, middle, or end).

3. Write out a lesson plan. Notice the kind of notes and shorthand that you use.

4. Share the plan with a classmate or colleague. Suggest to your partner a few things you would do differently, and listen to his or her suggestions for your own plan. Note that this doesn't mean you disagree with each other's plans. Anything can be taught in different ways. You are looking for options.

6. Assessing intermediate learners

In the previous chapter, we talked about some of the basics of assessment. With learners at an intermediate level, you may want to consider a wider range of ways to assess their progress. In this section, we're going to talk about three: self-assessment, communicative tests, and performance-based testing. These types of assessment often require higher language proficiency, so intermediate learners are more easily able to demonstrate their abilities with them.

Look back at the pages on evaluation on pages 82–83. Pay particular attention to the feedback form (page 83). Then answer the questions below.

1. How could a teacher use the information contained in the form to help make the class better?

2. How could learners use the information contained in the form to help their learning?

Before we go any further, we need to clear up some potential confusion in our terms. We used the word *evaluation* earlier in the chapter and in this section, we are going to talk about *assessment.* Nunan (2004, p. 138) sees *evaluation* as the larger term, "a broad set of procedures involving the collection and interpretation of information for curricular decision-making." The ways of collecting this information he calls assessment. Others use the two words interchangeably. What Rost calls evaluation in his list of strategies, we're going to call *self-assessment* and leave the matter alone.

Self-assessment can take many forms. In self-assessment, we often ask learners if they're comfortable with their linguistic abilities in terms of **functional language** (*I can talk about my life and family. I can ask for and give advice.*) and in terms of the grammar presented in the book (*I know more about how to use simple and first conditionals*). We can also find out what they think about their strategy use (*I know how to improve my listening.*). These questions are a little bit different from those that ask how the class is going (rating whether a listening lesson was useful/interesting/easy), but both kinds of questions are important.

Some teachers have a problem with **self-assessment** because it "only" asks what the learners think. It asks, for example, if they think they can ask for and give advice. It doesn't test their ability to do so. True enough. That's why any assessment plan requires multiple measures—many points of reference. We still need to give tests, but we can't ignore the students' perspectives, especially in listening, where it is so difficult to see what is going on in the learners' minds. Self-assessment allows us to see, somewhat at least, into the process the learners are going through. Another aspect of self-assessment that is important is its attention to how learners are feeling. Language learning is an emotional experience. We're taken back to childhood, in a sense; we cannot communicate in the sophisticated ways we can in our first languages. It's important for students, and teachers, to monitor their feelings as well as their linguistic accomplishments as they learn.

How does this apply specifically to listening materials? Example 12 is the "Check your progress" section of *Tapestry: Listening and Speaking 3.* Goals are set at the beginning of each chapter, there are a number of activities that help learners reach those goals, and then they are asked at the end of the chapter to take this survey.

Example 12

On a scale of 1 to 5, rate how well you have mastered the goals set at the beginning of the chapter:

1	2	3	4	5	use specific methods to communicate effectively with people from other cultures
1	2	3	4	5	use appropriate language to solve problems
1	2	3	4	5	recognize and use direct speech
1	2	3	4	5	recognize and use subtle speech
1	2	3	4	5	contribute your ideas in group activities

If you've given yourself a 3 or lower on any of these goals:

• visit the *Tapestry* website for additional practice.
• ask your instructor for extra help.
• review the sections of the chapter that you found difficult.
• work with a partner or study group to further your progress.

Tapestry: Listening and Speaking 3 (Carlisi and Christie, 2000)

Surveys like this are good quick indicators of student progress. Another way for teachers to monitor students' progress through self-assessment is by asking learners to keep journals, diaries, or learning logs. The teacher can ask one question (*What did you do this week to improve your English?*) that everyone is expected to answer or alternatively, the teacher can develop a form that learners can fill out each week or two. Example 13 (page 92) is a filled-in example from a Hong Kong Chinese student from Nunan (1996).

Example 13

Probe	At the beginning of the course	At the end of the course
This week I studied:	The nature of verbs.	I read a journal article called Geographic which is published in New Zealand. I have spent an hour to discussion with my psychology classmates.
This week I learned:	Some more information about English in English linguistics lesson.	The principles of morphology. How to use the self-access centre for learning English.
This week I used my English in these places:	Tutorials. My German lessons.	In the library, Knowles building, KK Leung building. At home. Along the street near my home.
This week I spoke English with these people:	History lecturer, EAS classmates and tutor, linguistics tutor	A foreigner—he asked me where is Lok Fu MTR station. The waiter in Mario restaurant.
This week I made these mistakes:	Using incorrect words.	I spent too much time watching tv while answering questions; I created a word "gesturally."
My difficulties are:	Lack of time.	Understanding the theme of a topic or an article. Writing fluent English essays.
I would like to know:	How to improve my English.	The method that can improve both my listening and speaking skills.
I would like help with:	Dictionaries.	Ensuring I would spend some time on reading but not on other leisure activities. Communicating with foreigners. Watching foreign films. Human resources that can improve my language ability.
My learning and practising plans for next week are:	To talk more.	To speak up in class and to use English to ask about anything I don't understand in any of my subjects. To try to understand by explaining to my schoolmates some topics of the essay before writing it.

Learner Strategy Training in the Classroom (Nunan in *TESOL Journal 6*, 1996, p. 96)

So far in this book, we have stressed the importance of tasks in teaching listening. Task-based listening is one part of the general trend toward communicative language teaching. Another part of that trend is the use of **communicative tests**. Communicative tests make an effort to simulate what learners are required to do in the real world, so usually they are a mix of listening and speaking (because you seldom only listen or only speak). At intermediate and advanced levels, this might take the form of, for example, hearing some information and sharing it with others to solve a problem (what is sometimes called **jigsaw listening**). A very common form of communicative test is the interview. Teachers talk to students one-on-one about the topics that have been studied in the textbook. A third kind of communicative test is pair- or group-work based. In Example 14, learners play a speaking game based on topics from the textbook. The way to make this a test is to place a tape recorder in the middle of the group (or have them play the game in a language laboratory with recording capacity). The teacher then listens to the tape and evaluates the students based on a list of class objectives.

Example 14

SUPPLEMENTARY MATERIALS

Activation:
a speaking and listening game

- Work in groups of 3 or 4.
- Each player puts a place marker on *Start here.*
- Close your eyes. Touch the *How many spaces?* box. Move that many spaces.
- Read the sentences. How much can you say about the topic?
- Each partner asks one question about what you said.
- Take turns.

When you have to make a difficult decision, who do you talk to?

Tell about a time you saw something surprising.

Start here

Think of a time you met someone from another country. What did you say? What did the other person say?

Did you believe in ghosts when you were younger? Do you now? Have you ever seen one?

Think of a poem in your language. Can you say it – or explain it – in English?

What is something you believed as a child but don't believe now?

If you could have a date with a famous person, who would it be? Why?

What story did you love when you were a child?

What topics do you usually talk about when you meet someone? What don't you talk about?

What was a very difficult decision to make?

Who's your hero? Why?

Tell about an

If you could change something about your personality, what would it be?

What don't you like to do to learn English?

What's the most unusual food you've ever eaten?

You can ask any player one question.

What's a custom in your country that is hard for foreigners to understand? How could you explain it?

What do you do for the environment? What else could you do?

What song has a special meaning for you? Why?

What's that m believe

Tell about an advertisement or a commercial you think is really good. Why do you think so?

How many spaces?					
2	1	3	1	3	2
1	3	4	2	3	1
3	1	2	1	2	3
1	2	1	3	5	2
3	5	2	1	2	3
2	1	3	4	3	1

What do people do that you think is very rude? What would you like to say to them? Do you?

What are five words or phrases that describe your personality?

Do you know of a custom from another country that you like? What is it?

What food is becoming more popular in your area?

Anyone can ask you one question.

What do you listen to in English? How many different things can you list?

What would make your area a better place to live?

Have you ever made a mistake that was funny or embarrassing?

What is your idea for "the perfect date"?

Would you rather be a boss or work for someone else? Why?

Have you ever had a pet? Tell about it. If you haven't, would you like one? What kind?

If you could have seen an important event in history, what would it be?

Does new technology make your life easier or more difficult?

What helps you learn English?

Tell about a sound you'll never forget.

Have you ever seen a piece of art that you thought was wonderful?

Do you do anything to bring good luck?

66

67

Active Listening 3 (Helgesen, Brown, and Smith, 1996, pp. 66–67)

These sorts of tests share some characteristics with **performance-based testing**. Performance-based testing differs slightly from communicative testing in that while communicative testing tries to simulate what goes on in the real world through pair and group work or through interviews with the teacher, performance-based testing (in its strictest form, at least) usually tries to directly assess the learner's skills. For example, if the class has been focused on travel English, the test might be a role play in which the teacher is a customs officer and the student a traveler. The grade for the test would be based on how well the student answers "the officer's" questions. Really the difference here is between **direct** and **indirect testing**. How closely do you want to come, in your test, to what the learners will do once they leave the classroom? In some situations, where the class is focused on a particular goal and certain set of skills, this is important. In a more general English class, you may be most concerned about the learner's overall proficiency, and in that case, more general tasks are appropriate.

7. Conclusion

Much of what we've looked at in the unit is aimed at giving the learners, as well as the teacher, more control of how they deal with what they are listening to. Though we should try to give learners control at all levels, intermediate learners are ready to take the step to assume even more control. By looking at what makes a listening text easy or difficult, we are able to manipulate it so learners can achieve success and the upward push that is the right level of challenge. By teaching and practicing listening strategies, the learners have more control over how they make sense of input. By adding a form-focused step after learners understand a meaning of the text, we can help them acquire the language. And by teaching them to go a bit beyond the main tasks, we help them take charge of their own understanding.

 Further readings

The following two books are practical, readable guides for ESL and EFL teachers. They contain short (usually 7–10 pages) summaries of major issues in teaching, including listening. New teachers will appreciate the concise summaries of each area. More experienced teachers can use the books as a way of keeping up with issues and trends.

Carter, R. and D. Nunan. 2002. *Teaching English to Speakers of Other Languages.* Cambridge, UK: Cambridge University Press.

Richards, J. and W. Renadya. 2002. *Methodology in Language Teaching: An Anthology of Current Practice.* Cambridge, UK: Cambridge University Press.

Helpful Web site

Dave's ESL café (www.eslcafe.com)

This is a very popular and easy to use site. One popular feature is the teacher discussion area where teachers talk about challenges and successes in their classrooms. It usually has a very helpful, supportive atmosphere. There is also an "idea cookbook" with usable activities, sorted by topic, including over 50 for listening passages.

References

American Council on the Teaching of Foreign Languages. 1986. ACTFL Proficiency Guidelines. Hasting-on-Hudson, NY: American Council on the Teaching of Foreign Languages.

Anderson, A. and T. Lynch. 1988. *Listening.* Oxford, UK: Oxford University Press.

Buck, G. 2001. *Assessing Listening.* Cambridge, UK: Cambridge University Press.

Carlisi, K. and S. Christie. 2000. *Tapestry 3 Listening & Speaking.* Boston: Heinle & Heinle.

Farrell, T. 2002. Lesson Planning. In Richards, J. and W. Renandya (eds.) *Methodology in Language Teaching: An Anthology of Current Practice.* Cambridge, UK: Cambridge University Press. 30–39.

Flowerdew, J. and L. Miller. 2005. *Second Language Listening.* Cambridge, UK: Cambridge University Press.

Freeman, D., K. Graves, and L. Lee. 2005. *ICON 2.* New York, NY: McGraw-Hill.

Gershon, S. and C. Mares. 2000. *Sound Bytes 2.* Hong Kong, PRC: Longman Asia ELT.

Harmer, J. 1998. *How to Teach English.* Harlow, UK: Addison Wesley Longman.

Harsch, K. and K. Wolfe-Quintero. 2001. *Impact Listening 3.* Hong Kong, PRC: Longman Asia ELT.

Helgesen, M., S. Brown, and T. Mandeville. 2004. *English Firsthand 2.* Hong Kong: Longman Asia ELT.

Helgesen, M., S. Brown, and D. Smith. 1996. *Active Listening 3: Expanding Understanding through Content*. Cambridge, UK: Cambridge University Press.

Helgesen, M., S. Brown, and D. Smith. 1996. *Active Listening 3 Teacher's Manual*. Cambridge, UK: Cambridge University Press.

Lynch, T. and J. Maclean. 2001. A case of exercising: Effects of Immediate Task Repetition on Learners' Performance. In M. Bygate, P. Skehan, and M. Swain (eds.) *Researching pedagogic tasks: Second Language Learning, Teaching and Testing*. Harlow, UK: Longman (Pearson Education).

Maley, A. 2000. Beating around the Bush. In Watcyn-Jones, P. (ed.) *Top Class Activities 2* Harlow, UK: Penguin/Pearson Education.

Murphey, T. 1998. *Language Hungry*. Tokyo, Japan: Macmillan Language House.

Murphey, T. 2001. Exploring Conversational Shadowing. *Language Teaching Research 5,* 2, 128–155.

Nunan, D. 1996. Learner Strategy Training in the Classroom: An Action Research Study. *TESOL Journal 6,* 1. 35–41.

Nunan, D. 2003. *Listen In Book 3* (2nd ed.) Boston, MA: Heinle/Thomson.

Nunan, D. 2004. *Task-Based Language Teaching*. Cambridge, UK: Cambridge University Press.

Oxford, R.L. 1990. *Language Learning Strategies. What Every Teacher Should Know*. New York, NY: Newbury House.

Richards, J. 2005. Second Thoughts on Teaching Listening. *RELC Regional Language Centre Journal* 36.1. 85–92.

Richards, J. and R. Schmidt. 2002. *Longman Dictionary of Language Teaching and Applied Linguistics*. Harlow, UK: Pearson Education.

Rost, M. 2002. *Teaching and Researching Listening*. Harlow, UK: Pearson Education/Longman.

Chapter **Four**

Listening for advanced level learners

1. Introduction

In this chapter, we explore aspects of teaching listening to advanced students. The chapter follows a structure similar to the last two chapters. We will first look at syllabus issues before discussing key concepts in the teaching of listening to advanced learners. Next, we will discuss the practicalities of teaching listening to advanced learners by looking at methods and materials. We will then move on to looking at classroom interaction. Finally, we look at how to assess advanced learners.

2. Syllabus design issues

What is "advanced" listening ability? The ACTFL proficiency guidelines for listening say that a person at the advanced level of proficiency should be able to understand:

- main ideas and most details.
- speech about a variety of topics, including those beyond the immediate situation. That is, learners should be able to follow a story if the speaker suddenly changes time frames.
- interviews, short lectures if the topic is familiar, and factual reports such as the news.

However, the guidelines say that advanced listeners may still not be able to understand texts that are very culturally specific or that have a lot of words with cultural references.

Reflection

1. Look at the definition of the advanced listener above. Think of your own language learning. If you have experienced actually using a second or foreign language outside of a language class, what things were you able to do at an advanced level—or what things would you still like to be able to do, but can't?

2. Do you have any advice for teachers of advanced students?

Share your answers with a classmate or colleague.

The ACTFL definition of an advanced listener raises at least three very broad syllabus issues. One issue is the **discourse** issue. This is shorthand for the fact that advanced learners still need to improve their abilities to understand longer pieces of text (interviews, lectures, news stories, etc.). You see this most concretely in classrooms with students whose goals are to attend a university in an English-speaking country (or one in which English is the language of instruction). In terms of academic listening skills, these students need to understand lectures and participate in discussions. Of course, these students also need to be able to survive in an English-speaking country, if that's their situation, and so they benefit from classroom instruction that extends their basic communicative abilities.

Reflection

Example 1 (pages 99–100) is the scope and sequence for an advanced level textbook that teaches academic listening and speaking. How is it different from the materials we have seen in the previous chapters? How is it similar? Is "discourse" (longer pieces of text) being taught?

Example 1

Chapter	Listening/Speaking Strategies	Mechanics/Academic Strategies
1	• guessing meaning from context • preparing to listen to a lecture • having questions in mind • taking lecture notes • synthesizing information	• telling a story • understanding reduced forms of words • psyching out your professors
2	• listening for implicit reasons • taking lecture notes	• expressing an opinion • expressing agreement or disagreement • softening disagreement • the voiceless *th* sound • using abbreviations
3	• understanding the passive voice • hearing rhyme and rhythm • giving a speech to the class • listening to a speech or presentation	• statements and questions • questions with *or* • responding to a negative question: agreeing • responding to a negative question: disagreeing • the medial *t* • making appointments/negotiating time • understanding common abbreviations • getting the main ideas in a lecture
4	• guessing meaning from context • finding a synopsis in the conclusion to a lecture	• starting a conversation • review: question intonation • reduced forms of *wh*- questions • the voiced /ð/ sound • organizing lecture notes graphically • comparing lecture notes

(Continued)

Chapter	Listening/Speaking Strategies	Mechanics/Academic Strategies
5	• managing a conversation • guessing the meaning of proverbs from context • listening for supporting statistics • listening for digressions • listening for quoted material • asking questions after a presentation	• tone of voice that changes meaning • giving advice and suggestions in the present • giving advice and suggestions for a past time • reduced forms in expressions for giving advice and suggestions • understanding Latin terms
6	• listening for indirect causes • listening to numerical information • reviewing what you already know/realizing what you don't know • giving a report from notes	• asking for confirmation • offering an explanation • tag question intonation • reduced forms of words in tag questions • choosing a topic
7	• listening to an anecdote • listening for topic signals • making eye contact	• answering the phone • finding out who's calling • taking a phone message • asking for clarification/clarifying • *can* and *can't* • recording an outgoing message • using a variety of sources and synthesizing information
8	• listening for emotions • recognizing figurative language • taking turns • listening to accented English	• expressing concern • intensifying concern • intensifying with stress • /ɛ/, /æ/, and /ə/ • memorizing

Quest 3: Listening and Speaking (Hartmann and Blass, 2000, pp. xvii–xviii)

The second big issue that teachers of advanced learners face is culture. As ACTFL notes, even advanced students cannot always understand the hidden meanings of individual words or phrases, and these hidden meanings may cause misunderstandings. These hidden meanings are the **connotations** of the word, the meanings that are not attached to the dictionary meaning. For example, learners might encounter the word *crazy*. They might look it up in the dictionary. We did (see Figure 1) and found that the dictionary said the word was used to talk about someone who is psychologically disturbed or who doesn't show good sense, or who is very fond of something (crazy about chocolate).

The dictionary doesn't say—and to be fair that's not the dictionary's job—that *crazy* has a lot of connotations. First of all, it's considered a very rude word when used to refer to mentally ill people, and people wouldn't use it in public speaking. Second, for Americans of a certain age, the word almost automatically brings up associations with a particular comedian, Steve Martin, who long ago called himself "a wild and crazy guy." For other Americans, it's difficult not to think of an old song called "Crazy." The list could go on, but the point is that words are never simply what they seem, and learners who really want to understand the language eventually learn to go beyond the dictionary and participate in the culture. They need to develop a kind of **cultural literacy**.

> **cra·zy** /kráyzee/ *adj* (**-zi-er, -zi-est**) **1** : UNBALANCED affected by psychological disturbance or instability, or produced by an unbalanced mind **2** : RIDICULOUS not showing good sense or practicality (*informal*) **3** : EXCESSIVELY FOND excessively fond of somebody or something (*informal*) *n* (*plural* **-zies**) UNBALANCED PERSON somebody whose behavior shows signs of psychological disturbance or instability (*informal*) —**cra·zi·ly** *adv* —**cra·zi·ness** *n*

Figure 1: Definition of *crazy* from *Encarta World English Dictionary* (Soukhanov, 1999)

Of course, even at advanced levels, problems other than the meanings of words can provide challenges and misunderstandings. For example, a few years ago when we were writing a series of listening textbooks, one of us mentioned to the listening lab technician that we wanted to teach a pilot version of the book and wondered if her lab was available. The technician, a Japanese woman with an advanced degree in English and a very competent speaker of the language, looked at us gravely, "You're authors. You know you should not have a pirate edition of a book." In her case, despite her good English, phonological interference from her first language caused misunderstanding. Other factors such as culture, grammar, and vocabulary can lead to problems. Even at the most advanced levels, learners need to be checking their own comprehension as they listen.

There are other cultural challenges for learners, of course. We noted in Chapter 1 that there are different modes of listening—overhearing people talk on a tape, listening to a lecture, and listening and responding to another person in a conversation. How people respond to others when they are talking is very cultural and to be a good listener means to be an appropriate listener. Americans and Japanese differ, for example, on how much feedback or **back channeling** (using phrases such as *Uh huh* and *Really?*) to give to people they're talking to. It's polite in Japan to let the speaker know you're listening by saying short phrases or words while listening. It's also polite in the United States, but the amount of back channeling is less.

One way to teach culture is through **authentic texts**, which is the third big syllabus issue for advanced learners. By *authentic* we mean materials not made for language teaching, for example, real TV programs and not videos made especially to teach language. By *texts* we mean what we listen to as well as what we read. Authenticity has become an important idea in **Communicative Language Teaching**. The issue is often presented as *either/or*. Either a text is authentic or it's not—and authentic texts, according to some, are the only sorts of texts that learners need. Learners, in this view, should only listen to authentic materials—radio, TV, movies, songs. But, in our opinion, authenticity is not either/or, and in fact sometimes authentic texts are just too difficult for learners. In fact, text authenticity is more like a rainbow than black and white. Brown and Menasche (2005) say there are five types of text authenticity.

- **Genuine text authenticity**. The text is created for some real-life purpose, not for the classroom. However, it is used in English teaching. No changes at all are made in the text. For example, an entire radio feature may be listened to without interruption and without consulting the script (an example of listening for pleasure).
- **Altered text authenticity**. The text hasn't been changed in meaning, but it is no longer exactly as it was because of changes made for the classroom. For example, most teachers probably break up a long (8–10 minute) radio feature into short segments, with vocabulary work and discussion following each segment, rather than playing the whole thing at once.
- **Adapted text authenticity**. The text was originally created for "real life" but has been adapted by the classroom teacher. Words and grammatical structures are changed, usually to simplify the text. This happens sometimes when textbook writers base their tasks on real news reports, for example, but rewrite the reports in a more understandable form for lower level learners. This is sometimes called an **elaborated text**. The information is "authentic" but the form is not.
- **Simulated text authenticity**. The text is created for the classroom and is written by the author or teacher *as if* the material were real and *as if* for a real audience. This differs from an adapted text because in this case the information is not necessarily authentic.
- **Inauthentic texts**. The text is created for the classroom with no attempt to make the materials resemble genuine authentic materials. It is important to note that 'inauthentic' materials are not necessarily bad. Word lists are inauthentic, for example, but they, in the right circumstances, might be useful for language learning.

Beyond the listening texts, we also need to look at the levels of authenticity in listening tasks themselves. Nunan (2004, p. 1) notes that there is a difference between real-world or **target tasks** (tasks learners will do with their language once they leave class) and **pedagogical tasks**, "those that occur in the classroom." Brown and Menasche (2005) use different terms and see these three types of task authenticity: genuine, simulated, and pedagogical.

- **Genuine task authenticity**. This exists when learners do tasks in ways and for reasons they would in the real world. For example, a listening center in the classroom may offer students a chance to view DVDs, listen to CDs, or surf the Internet, without making any specific demands that the learners complete an assignment.
- **Simulated task authenticity**. In simulated task authenticity, there is some attempt to copy real life within the context of the classroom, but

the focus is on language learning. Asking learners to extend a conversation they have heard by role playing the characters and figuring out what might have happened next in the conversation is an example of a simulated task—one whose purpose is language learning, but that at least partially mirrors the real world.

- **Pedagogical task authenticity**. This occurs when there is no attempt to copy real life, but the task is useful within the context of the classroom. For example, learners may well benefit from a task that asks them to listen and discriminate between sets of numbers like *fifteen* and *fifty*. It's not authentic to listen to a list of numbers and choose which one is being said, but it can be a useful form of practice that can be applied to real-life situations later, for instance while shopping.

Look at several listening exercises in this book or in a text you have used for teaching or studying.

1. What kind of *task* and *text* authenticity does each task represent?

2. Do the exercises cover a full range of task and text authenticity or are they limited? If they are limited, do you feel that is useful (for simplicity, "teachability," or other reasons) or is it a bad thing? Why?

Share your ideas with a classmate or colleague.

3. Principles for teaching listening to advanced learners

It would be wrong to say that teaching listening to advanced learners, as opposed to teaching beginning or intermediate learners, involves a change in tactics or in content. Just as you can't simply put another story on a house without reinforcing and strengthening the underlying frame, you can't just add on academic content to a listening class and call it an advanced class. Learners will need to continue to work on their basic communication skills. That's why our first principle is: Build on what learners already know about listening.

1. Build on what learners already know about listening.

We suggested in Chapter 2 that tasks like **TPR (Total Physical Response)** and raising hands to indicate when learners heard a particular word were appropriate for beginners. As teachers, we sometimes think we should put the old tasks aside and move on to tasks appropriate for advanced students (note-taking, perhaps). However, this is not always the case. Often we only need to increase the difficulty of the text. Consider a telephone conversation with the technical support people at a software company. You have a problem, and they're trying to talk you through the solution—a TPR task in which you follow instructions and correct the problem. This is not as easy as it sounds, depending on your level of computer expertise. If you know only the basics about computers, and the other person is an expert without good skills in talking to people who aren't computer experts, you'll probably become very frustrated by trying to do this sophisticated listening task.

For another example, see Example 2, a task from an advanced textbook.

Example 2

Listening

Jessica Drake is one of Hollywood's top dialect coaches. Her job is to help actors add or remove accents according to the requirements of the movie or TV show. She's worked with actors such as Pierce Brosnan, Keanu Reeves, and Meg Ryan. She's reduced French accents and created Swedish ones. Drake explains just how she does her job.

Global Listening

Read the following list of topics. As you listen to the interview for the first time, mark an X on the line next to the ideas that Jessica Drake talks about.

_____ the process of teaching an actor to use an accent

_____ designing a dialect for the movie Forrest Gump

_____ why there are many different accents spoken in the American South

_____ how a character in a film and an accent develop together

_____ how Forrest Gump's dialect sounded

_____ the accent used by other characters in Forrest Gump

_____ how long it takes an actor to learn a dialect

_____ funny stories about actors learning dialects

_____ the effect an accent has on an actor's body language

_____ qualities a good dialect coach must have

Now, compare your answers with those of a partner.

Talk it Over: Listening, Speaking and Pronunciation (Kozyrev, 2002, p. 60)

Notice that the only task the learners are required to do in Example 2 is check the main topics the speaker talks about. This listening text is an interview with a dialect coach, who helps actors use the correct regional accent in movies. The interview is sophisticated in its vocabulary and ideas, which may be new to learners. In terms of text, it's clearly at an advanced level, but all the learners do is make checks. After all, it's a listening task, not a writing task. If learners check the correct topics, they've understood. We should also note that while checking a box may indeed show understanding, the gap between the level of response required and the level of the text could end up being frustrating.

Example 3 is the next task in the unit. It requires learners to take notes using a specific method. Notice the task is quite **open-ended**: "Listen again to the interview with Jessica Drake, and take notes by using the Cornell method of note-taking. Use your notes to answer the questions on the next page." There is no "correct" answer. Learners are experiencing a similar freedom of response as they would if they were taking notes for their own purposes.

Example 3

Note Taking

In this chapter, you will practice a style of note taking that was developed at Cornell University. Read the following description of the Cornell method of note taking, then listen again to the interview with Jessica Drake and take notes using this method.

The Cornell Method

To use this method of note taking, draw a line about one-third of the distance from the left edge of the page. (See the example, below.) Take notes on the right side of the line. Use the space to the left of the line to write main ideas, important words, terms being defined, and questions answered in the body of the notes. You can save time and be more accurate by filling in the left side of the page after you have finished taking notes.

General description of her job	Remove or establish accent for a group, or one actor Many dialects are in demand, filmmakers want realism

Talk it Over: Listening, Speaking and Pronunciation (Kozyrev, 2002, p. 61)

In Example 3, the kinds of difficulties learners will face are different from the previous task in Example 2. They've already heard the interview once, so listening to it this time will be easier. In terms of the task, they are faced with the challenge not only of taking notes, but also of using a style of note-taking that has just been introduced to them.

Therefore, one difference between beginning and advanced levels has to do with the required tasks as well as the texts the learners hear, yet it is also true that advanced learners are able to do more things. One of those things is to make better use of more sophisticated **learning strategies**. (For more about learning strategies, see pages 65–68.) Advanced learners can also participate in more sophisticated conversations that require them to be active listeners.

As we have seen, learners should be taught to make use of strategies from the very beginning. However, the balance of strategies that are used may change over time as language students become more skilled, and certainly the way students can talk about the strategies changes. Advanced learners need to know how to use **metacognitive strategies**. Metacognitive strategies require students to think about their learning, organize it, and reflect on it.

Keeping track of learning is often done by keeping a learning journal. This journal can be taped or written. At different points of time in the course, or maybe more often, like once week, students are asked to think about their learning. What has been easy? What has been difficult? How can they do better? They write down their responses to these questions, or speak their answers into a tape recorder.

Another metacognitive strategy is planning. Planning asks learners to think about their learning. What do they want to learn? How are they going to do it? Beginning and intermediate students can use these strategies, but it takes a certain proficiency in English to be able to use English to report on their use. Advanced students have this proficiency.

We'll say again that listening is not only listening to an audio program that comes with a textbook. Listening is done when students work with others in pairs and groups and when they listen to the teacher. Students have been talking as well as listening throughout their English studies. As beginners, they often had conversations that sounded more like police interrogations than anything else:

> *Question:* What's your name?
> *Answer:*   Pilar.
> *Question:* Where are you from?
> *Answer:*   Mexico City.
> *Question:* What sports do you like?
> *Answer:*   Tennis.

As students become more proficient in English, they need to learn ways to have smoother conversations, to listen to what their partner says, to answer questions with other questions, and to generally become more active in keeping a conversation going. Many textbooks now try to help students do this. Example 4 gives learners ways to actively participate in a conversation about controversial issues.

Example 4

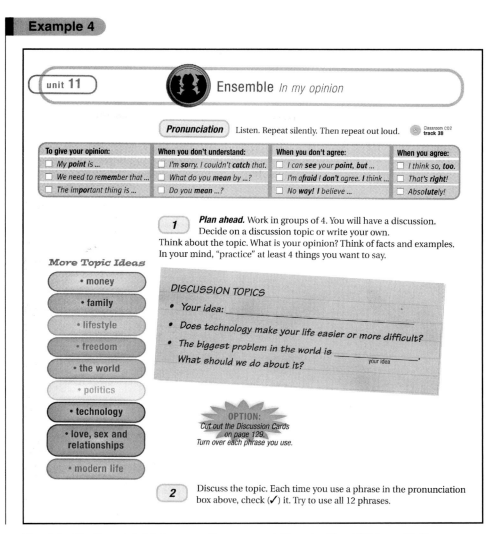

Ensemble *In my opinion*

Pronunciation Listen. Repeat silently. Then repeat out loud. Classroom CD2 track 38

To give your opinion:	When you don't understand:	When you don't agree:	When you agree:
☐ My **point** is ...	☐ I'm **sorry**. I couldn't **catch** that.	☐ I can **see** your **point, but** ...	☐ I think so, **too**.
☐ We need to **remember** that ...	☐ What do you **mean** by ...?	☐ I'm **afraid** I **don't** agree. I think ...	☐ That's **right**!
☐ The **important** thing is ...	☐ Do you **mean** ...?	☐ No **way**! I believe ...	☐ **Absolute**ly!

1 **Plan ahead.** Work in groups of 4. You will have a discussion. Decide on a discussion topic or write your own.
Think about the topic. What is your opinion? Think of facts and examples. In your mind, "practice" at least 4 things you want to say.

More Topic Ideas

- money
- family
- lifestyle
- freedom
- the world
- politics
- technology
- love, sex and relationships
- modern life

DISCUSSION TOPICS

- Your idea: _____
- Does technology make your life easier or more difficult?
- The biggest problem in the world is _____
  What should we do about it? *your idea*

OPTION:
Cut out the Discussion Cards on page 129.
Turn over each phrase you use.

2 Discuss the topic. Each time you use a phrase in the pronunciation box above, check (✓) it. Try to use all 12 phrases.

English Firsthand 2 (Helgesen, Brown, and Mandeville, 2004, p. 104)

2. Teach the culture as well as the language.

We said earlier in this chapter that even advanced learners may have trouble understanding certain conversations or texts because of cultural information the learners may not have. Many advanced textbooks use authentic radio or television programs to teach listening skills. Example 5 (page 108) is a task that uses an advertisement for an airline.

Example 5

🔊 Listen to the Northwest Airlines Ad

Take Notes

DIRECTIONS: You are going to hear the radio advertisement for Northwest Airlines. Take notes on a separate sheet of paper as you listen. Write down main ideas, details, or any words that will help you discuss the ad.

🔊 Listen Again to the Northwest Airlines Ad

Check What You Hear

DIRECTIONS: Rewind the tape and listen again to the ad for Northwest Airlines. Following are sentences from the tape in the order that you will hear them. There are also some sentences that are not on the tape. Listen carefully, and when you hear one of the sentences, put a check (✓) beside it.

1. ___ Before you book a flight for Asia.

2. ___ Is this the most comfortable way to get there?

3. ___ You can get to Asia up to five hours faster.

4. ___ Fly from beautiful California.

5. ___ The connection is quick and convenient.

6. ___ There's more personal space.

7. ___ The food is delicious.

8. ___ [You have] your own personal video system.

9. ___ Call your travel agent.

10. ___ Some people just know how to fly.

DISCUSS THE MEANING OF EACH SENTENCE. THEN GO BACK AND LISTEN AGAIN TO THE AD FOR NORTHWEST AIRLINES.

Check Your Understanding

🔊 True or False

DIRECTIONS: Decide whether the following seven phrases used to complete the sentence are true or false according to the information you have heard in the ad for Northwest Airlines. Mark T (for true) or F (for false) for each phrase.

According to the advertisement, there are advantages for getting to Asia on Northwest Airlines from the United States if you

1. ___ live in New York City.

2. ___ live in Los Angeles.

3. ___ live in Miami.

4. ___ enjoy classical music.

5. ___ need more space for sleeping.

On the Air: Listening to Radio Talk (Sadow and Sather, 1998, pp. 56–57)

These advanced textbooks that use authentic radio programs don't always explicitly teach about the culture, but they do assume that by listening to what native speakers of English listen to, learners will acquire vocabulary and background knowledge that will help them better understand authentic materials, in part by helping them develop cultural literacy. This is a major reason such materials are often used at the advanced level.

These books also assume that English language learners will be interested in topics Americans are interested in. In our experience, this is not always true. Students do like to listen to radio, television, and other media, however. At the advanced level, assignments that ask students to listen outside of class work really well. (For ways that students can listen outside of class, see the section on autonomy in Chapter 5 (pages 136–142).)

3. Help learners understand the structure of longer texts.

Depending on the program they are enrolled in, learners may listen to long stretches of discourse from the very beginning. Their teachers may, for example, read or tell them stories. Often, however, schools may put off extended listening until the advanced level. And for many of these schools "extended listening" means listening to lectures. Though things are changing somewhat, most universities still use lectures, especially in introductory courses where they want to make sure all the students get the same information.

Understanding lectures requires several (Richards, 1985) "micro-skills."

Action

Can you do these things in a second language? If so, which are easy, medium difficult, and difficult? Write *E, M,* or *D* next to each micro-skill.

In order to understand lectures, learners need to be able to identify:

———— • what the lecture is about, in a wide sense. This allows learners to use their **schemata**.
———— • how the topic changes and develops over time.
———— • the main ideas and how they are connected to each other. This means that learners have to be able to understand what is a main idea and what is a detail that supports the main idea.
———— • the relationships between the different parts (cause and effect, main argument and conclusion).
———— • **discourse markers** like *on the other hand* and *another example*.
———— • what's important and when the topic changes. They can sometimes use the speaker's voice to figure these things out.
———— • special vocabulary related to the topic.
———— • the meaning of unknown words (by using context).
———— • the speaker's attitude toward the subject. Is the speaker joking, critical, angry?

Learners should also be able to recognize:

——— • the difference between things that are relevant and statements that are off the topic—jokes, stories, etc.

——— • body language such as gestures that the speaker might use to show that something is important.

——— • other ways that language is used in the classroom, for example, to give hints about what might be on the test, or to give advice in how to study.

Finally, since speakers will vary, learners need to be familiar with different styles of lecturing—formal, informal, planned, and unplanned (adapted from Richards 1985).

Share your answers with a classmate or colleague.

Once learners are familiar with these things, they must also be able to take good notes. Example 6 uses some of these tasks to help learners understand a lecture. Note that all these tasks are to be used before students begin listening.

Example 6

Taking Lecture Notes

It's important to take careful notes as you listen to a lecture because exam questions come not only from reading but also from lectures. You'll practice lecture note taking in every chapter of this book. Here are a few general suggestions:

· Don't "just listen" and not take notes at all. You won't remember the information in several weeks, at exam time, and there won't be anything you can study.

· Don't try to write everything. Note taking is not dictation!

· Don't write complete sentences. There probably won't be time.

· In your notes, try to distinguish general from specific points. One way to do this is to keep general points on the left. Indent a little to the right for more specific points. Indent further to the right for small details. A formal outline (as you see on pages 25–27) is one way to do this.

· Use abbreviations whenever possible.

· Predict which words will appear often in a lecture and decide on your *own* abbreviations for them.

D. Using Abbreviations. The following box contains some common abbreviations that students use. After the box is a list of words that you'll hear often in the lecture. Decide on your own abbreviations for each one.

Common Abbreviations			
about	abt	somebody	sbdy
and	+ or &	something	sthg
especially	esp	typical/typically	typ
essential	ess	with	w/
important	imp	without	w/out
means	=		

Words in the Lecture   My Abbreviations

1. shaman   _____

2. shamanism   _____

3. spirit   _____

Words in the Lecture	My Abbreviations
4. North America	_____
5. South America	_____
6. North American Indians	_____
7. psychology/psychologically	_____
8. transformed	_____
9. hallucinogenic	_____
10. patient (meaning a person)	_____
11. difficult	_____
12. ventriloquist*	_____

*Don't worry about this word. You'll probably be able to guess the meaning when you hear it in the lecture.

Listening

A. Vocabulary: Health and Healing. (Audio) Listen to the following words and terms in the context of sentences. Each one has a meaning in the list on the right. Write the letter of the meaning next to the word or term it matches.

Words/Terms	Meanings
_____ 1. at death's door	a. caused by drugs
_____ 2. ailing	b. almost dead
_____ 3. afflicted with	c. suffering from
_____ 4. suck	d. person who works in a profession, especially medicine
_____ 5. drug-induced	e. sick
_____ 6. consumption	f. eating or drinking
_____ 7. invalid	g. take into the mouth by using just the muscles of the mouth
_____ 8. practitioner	h. person weakened by illness

B. Listening for the Main Idea. (Audio) You'll hear a lecture called "Shamanism," written by an anthropology professor. Listen once to the entire lecture. (You'll listen again later.) As you listen this time, don't take notes. Instead, follow along with the outline and keep this question in mind:

• What are shamans, and how do they work?

Quest 3 Listening and Speaking (Hartmann and Blass, 2000, pp. 23–24)

4.   Tasks and materials

The purpose of this section is to describe and illustrate some task and activity types that can be used with advanced learners. These task and activity types (see Lund 1990 for more) include:

1. condensing
2. extending
3. modeling
4. conversing
5. songs, movies, TV, stories

1. Condensing

At an advanced level, students are often asked to listen to a text and write down its essentials. They may do this by taking notes, outlining, or writing a summary. Traditionally, advanced listening textbooks have taught how to take notes in a very straightforward way, usually by using an outline format. See Example 7.

Example 7

C. Taking Notes. **Audio**   Listen to the entire lecture again. This time fill in the outline.

Shamanism

Seventeenth century engraving of a shaman

I. What Are Shamans?
   A. The meaning of the word: _one who is excited or moved_

   B. Where shamanism is found: _____

   C. Who are shamans? _____

II. Shamans, The Individual, And The Community
   A. Why shamans are useful: _____

Quest 3 Listening and Speaking (Hartmann and Blass, 2000, p. 25)

However, not all students organize information in such a linear order, so textbooks have also begun teaching different styles of note-taking, using **graphic organizers** or **mind maps**. Example 8 is an example of a graphic organizer from the same textbook.

Example 8

American Folk Heroes

Folk heroes = heroes that slowly evolved and cannot be identified with a particular author

Am. situation: _____

Hero: _____

Info abt him:

Represents/Reflects:

Exploits explain:

Hero: _____

Info abt him:

Exploits explain/show:

Quest 3 Listening and Speaking (Hartmann and Blass, 2000, p. 127)

Example 9 (page 114) is an advanced level note-taking activity. It is based on a simulated television program about a British company that has incorporated ideas from Chinese *feng shui* into its factory. At the first listening, learners simply listen for the main elements (water, wood, etc.). After that, they listen for the qualities each element represents (wood = relaxing, fights stress). Finally, they listen to find out how each element is introduced into a building. Students are also asked to find out what the results in the factory are. As a follow-up, they can decide how to redesign their own classroom in light of what they learned.

Example 9

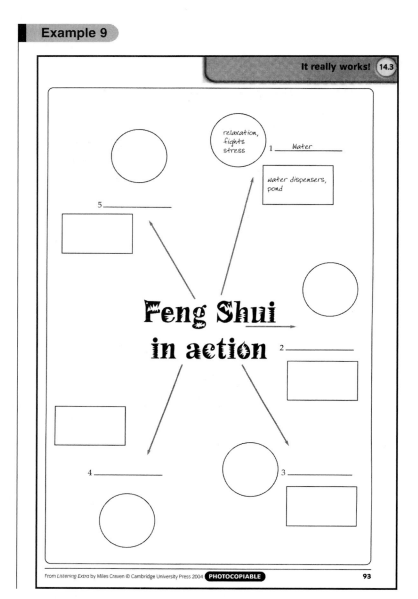

Listening Extra (Craven, 2004, p. 93)

2. Extending

Many books integrate listening and speaking activities. Example 10 is from a book which asks students to give their personal opinions of the topic they have just listened to. This is something teachers can do with any book or listening text, if the topic is interesting enough.

Example 10

■ **Real World Listening**

1 Predict

Sunhee is a Korean-American. She is calling for advice. She is planning to get married to a man from India. **What do you think she wants advice about?**

☐ whether she should marry him or not
☐ how they should deal with her parents
☐ how they should deal with his parents
☐ whether they should have children
☐ some other issues? _____

🎧 **Now listen and check your prediction.**

2 Get the main ideas

Which statements describe Sunhee's problem?

☐ Sunhee's parents live far away.
☐ Sunhee wants to have a child.
☐ Sunhee wants to get married.

☐ Sunhee's fiancé has a different religion.
☐ Sunhee's fiancé doesn't like her parents.
☐ Sunhee's parents want her to marry a Korean.

Which statements describe Carla's advice?

☐ Do what your parents want.
☐ Follow your heart.

☐ Have a child.
☐ Move back to your home country.

3 Respond to the ideas

1. Do you agree with Carla's advice? Would you give any different advice?
2. What are your views about international marriage?

Impact Listening 3 (Harsch and Wolfe-Quintero, 2001, p. 37)

3. Modeling

Another way to start a speaking activity is by using the listening as a model. This can be done at all levels. For example, at the beginning level, students may hear a dialogue and then practice it with a partner. At the advanced level, we'd probably want students to go beyond simply repeating. They might do a **role play**–where they are the characters in the dialogue–but use their own ideas, likes and dislikes, etc. to take the dialogue in a different direction so that the dialogue would likely be more sophisticated.

In Example 11 (page 116), learners have heard about a problem someone is having with telling a "white lie." They are supposed to do a role play in which they refuse an invitation not because they can't go, but because they don't want to go. They are given some conversation strategies to help accomplish their task.

Example 11

---

2 LISTENING: *A dilemma*

A. 🎧 FIRST LISTENING. Talk with a partner about what you see in the pictures. Then listen to the conversation and circle the answers to the questions.

1. Who has the dilemma?	**a.** Annie	**b.** Stephanie	**c.** Joo-chan
2. Who lies?	**a.** Annie	**b.** Stephanie	**c.** Joo-chan
3. Who acts ethically?	**a.** Annie	**b.** Stephanie	**c.** Joo-chan

B. 🎧 SECOND LISTENING. Listen again and answer the questions.

1. What is the dilemma? _____

_____

2. What is the lie? _____

_____

C. 🎧 ROLEPLAY. Listen and practice the conversations below. Then work with a partner to roleplay the following situation:

Your partner wants you to go somewhere with him/her, but you don't want to go. Tell your partner that you can't go and give an excuse.

> **CONVERSATION STRATEGY:** *Giving excuses*
>
> **I'd love to, but I can't. I have to . . .**   **I wish I could, but unfortunately I'm busy . . .**
> **Thank you, but I'm afraid I can't because . . .   Could I take a rain check on that?**
>
> **1.** A: Would you like to go to Daniel's party with us tonight?
>   B: **I'd love to, but I can't. I have to** study for a test tonight.
> **2.** A: If you're not busy tomorrow night, perhaps we could go to a movie together.
>   B: **Could I take a rain check on that?** I have other plans tomorrow night.
> **3.** A: I wonder if you could help me out with my homework tonight.
>   B: **I wish I could, but unfortunately I'm busy** tonight. I have to take care of an elderly aunt.

Icon 3 (Freeman, Graves, and Lee, 2005, p. 43)

4. Conversing

Once again we remind you that speaking activities are listening activities. When learners are speaking to each other, they are (we hope!) listening. The idea of listening as a social activity will be discussed more completely in Chapter 5.

5. Songs, Movies, TV, Stories

At any level, students appreciate songs, movies, and TV programs. As we've seen, at an advanced level, culture becomes an even more important part of the syllabus, and media are a great way to present culture. You can give students access to songs and movies in self-access centers (see autonomy section Chapter 5 (pages 136–142)), where they can listen and view for fun. You can make use of songs and stories in more traditional ways, using them as springboards for lessons about the language. We think that allowing students to just listen and enjoy is a great use of their time, however. Really understanding and appreciating a story is a very complex act of comprehension, too. It may look like fun, but it's a good language work-out, too.

5. Listening in the advanced classroom

This section will take a deeper look at how some of the tasks and materials presented in Section 4 might be used in a classroom. First, we'll look at Example 7 (p. 112) from this chapter to talk about the balance between preparation or pre-listening and actual listening. Then we'll look at Example 8 (p. 113) and talk about individual differences in the classroom. Finally, we'll look at Example 10 (p. 115) and how a textbook summarizes some of the themes we have talked about in this book.

In Example 7, we have shown the first page of three on which learners are supposed to take notes about an academic lecture on shamanism. A shaman is a kind of healer in certain societies. This page is part of a long chapter (26 pages) that uses the topic of shamanism. The purpose of the book is to prepare advanced learners to go to an English-using university. The book uses topics that students might study in introductory classes. This topic comes from an introductory cultural anthropology class. The lecture the learners hear is the fourth listening in the chapter. In the first listening, learners hear three students studying for an examination in their cultural anthropology class. In the second, they hear someone tell a personal story about their uncle's encounter with a shaman. In the third, they hear a radio interview with the author of a book on shamanism. Then they listen to an academic lecture as the fourth listening.

Note the variety of listening students are experiencing: a conversation, a story, an interview, and a lecture. The variety of tasks that students do, and the variety of texts they hear, is a big issue in academic listening. Finding the right mix of topics, texts, and tasks is important because academic English programs are often integrated. That means that the listening/speaking classes often concentrate on the same subjects as the reading/writing classes. If teachers teach closely to the book, even if it is a good book (and the book in our example is a good book), that is likely to become a problem. One solution is to get away from the book in every class. That means that the lesson is not integrated, that we don't spend the whole class period talking about one topic. In a class that combines speaking and listening, we might have a strand or mini-syllabus for pronunciation and a strand for everyday English in addition to a strand for academic English, so that we'd spend 10 minutes on pronunciation, 15 minutes on pair work using conversational English, and 20 minutes on academic English.

Another way to look at the balance of tasks is to look at the ratio of pre-listening to listening. In the chapter our example comes from, the students have heard three other pieces of audio, each with pre-listening and post-listening tasks—and that's very appropriate. Each listening needs pre-listening and post-listening of some sort. To get ready for the last task, listening to an academic lecture, they do other pre-listening activities, including: brainstorming what they know about shamanism based on what's come before in the chapter; previewing the pages on which they'll take notes; doing two vocabulary activities; reading about a few strategies for note-taking; and doing an exercise that teaches common abbreviations that note-takers use (*abt* for *about*, *sbdy* for *somebody*, etc.). At this point, teachers will need to make some decisions about which of these tasks to do as homework and which to do in class. In this case, the vocabulary exercises and the information about abbreviations would be good candidates for homework, but assigning pre-listening homework brings up yet another issue. We worked together once in a program where the students were supposed to prepare tasks in their academic vocabulary textbook at home, so that class time could be used for answering questions. Some students did the homework and others didn't. The teacher was then put in the position where half the class was "on the same page" and the other half was unprepared. The first couple of times this happens, you can pair a prepared student with an unprepared one and have one help the other. After a while, the prepared students feel resentful and the unprepared, rewarded for not studying, give up, so this is no long-term solution. We're not sure what the answer is (actually, we think the answer is motivation, but that's too huge a topic to address here), but we do know that finding a way for students to take some responsibility for some of the pre-listening tasks in academic textbooks, given their greater number than in other textbooks, is something teachers of advanced learners need to think about. For some classes, the answer may be that the students aren't ready for that responsibility and all the pre-listening needs to be done in class.

What is too much pre-listening? This is not a simple matter. Is it worthwhile to use 20 minutes for learners to do a task that teaches them, or reminds them that they know, the vocabulary necessary to understand a three-minute audio clip? Probably, if the vocabulary they're working with is useful for things beyond understanding the audio, which it likely will be. When we're teaching listening, we're teaching English as well.

Example 8 (p. 113) raises the issue of individual differences in the classroom. It presents a more visual way of taking notes than the ordinary outline. A lot of students learn visually and many learn in other ways (see Chapter 5, pp. 143–145). The key is to give opportunities to use different ways of learning in your class. You probably won't be able to use each type each day, but make sure there's a good mix. The question raised by Example 8 is whether to make every student try every way of learning. You could simply allow students to take notes in any way they wished. But as our mothers said when we wouldn't eat a new kind of vegetable, "How do you know you won't like it unless you try it?"

Another issue about individual differences is raised by thinking about how the notes will be graded, or what feedback teachers will give. This is an issue for any academic class and for any textbook. Our example book recommends, intelligently we think, that students develop their own abbreviations for note-taking (though they are given some suggestions). How then does the teacher give feedback to the whole class, with everyone using different abbreviations? What does the key, the correct answer, look like? This is something teachers of advanced learners will probably need to negotiate with the class.

Example 10 (p. 115) builds on a number of ideas in the book. It's a "Real World Listening" based on an interview with no script. It thus has a lot of "authenticity." It builds on what students already know because the topic is asking for and giving advice, which by this level they have studied several times. In fact, on the previous page, learners have listened to scripted recordings about problems and advice. Example 10 summarizes the model of pre-listening, while-listening, and post-listening we have seen several times. The pre-listening is a prediction activity. A Korean woman is calling a friend to ask for advice about marrying a man from India. The learner is asked to think about the kinds of advice she might want. They use their own life experiences, activate their schemata. By predicting, they are also engaged, interested in the activity. They're curious to see if they're correct. Then they listen for main ideas and check them. The level of response required is lower than the level of difficulty of the listening. Finally, they are asked two questions that require a personal response to the material. This is a good example of an advanced activity that tries to interest the learner by using real examples and a personal connection.

6. Assessing advanced learners

At the advanced level, some learners need to present norm-referenced (see page 20) assessment scores, either for educational or professional purposes. Learners who want to study at English-medium universities often take the Test of English as a Foreign Language (TOEFL®) offered by Educational Testing Service (ETS). International business people may need to take the Test of English for International Communication (TOEIC®), also offered by

ETS. Both of these tests are in a multiple-choice format. Universities and companies set a minimum score for admission or for getting promoted. It's really not our purpose here to analyze either test extensively. Both tests are very important to ESL and EFL students, so you'll need to know something about them.

As of 2005, ETS has begun to offer a new TOEFL. The listening section of the new test is somewhat different than the old one, yet many of the question types are the same. Learners hear either a rather long lecture on an academic subject or a conversation that might take place at a university—in a professor's office or at the library, for example. They may take notes on what they hear. (Incidentally, test-takers were not allowed to take notes during the "old" TOEFL, so in a sense, note-taking has become a more important skill to teach, at least to those learners who are planning to take this test.) They are then asked questions about main ideas and details, and inference questions about the speaker's purpose or attitude (*What does the professor mean? Why does he say this?*).

The TOEIC tests the skills of people who work for or want to work for international companies. Scores are often used as a job requirement. For example, a manager might have to get a certain score and a clerk another, lower, one. The TOEIC is also used to measure progress in company training programs. For example, it might be given at the beginning and the end of an English course to measure how effective the class was. The listening part of the test has four parts.

In the first part, test-takers must choose the sentence that best describes a picture. In the second, test-takers hear a question, and they must choose which response is best. In the third, they hear short conversations and answer questions about main ideas and details. In the fourth part, test-takers hear a short talk or announcement and answer questions about main ideas, details, and the purpose of the speaker.

Six hints for taking the listening part of the TOEIC

by Hiroshi Adachi, author of *How to Use English, The Nissan Way* (Kobunsha Paperbacks) and *Super Strategy for the TOEIC Test* (Chukei)

Hint 1: Don't try to listen to all the words and sentences!
Instead, just focus on content words, which include names, verbs, numbers, proper nouns, and negative words. Content words are essential for you to understand each dialogue's content and flow. By contrast, you can skip function words, which are not so seriously important for your listening comprehension. Function words include articles, relatives, *be*-verbs, and prepositions.

(continued)

Hint 2: Don't think about answers you have finished.

Instead, focus on the answer you are listening for now. Unfortunately, even if you think about the previous dialogue, you have no chance to listen to it again. Think of this as a mental game. If you want to win the TOEIC game, you have to overcome the temptation to keep worrying about the previous questions. Don't try to be perfect, but instead, try to shift your attention quickly.

Hint 3: Don't stop listening when facing unknown words.

Instead, just skip unfamiliar words and focus on familiar words such as people's names, numbers, days, days of the week, the name of places and so on. In general, the TOEIC test does not test your vocabulary comprehension for very high level words or overly specific technical terms.

Hint 4: In Part III and Part IV of the test, don't choose answers including the exact word you heard in the dialogues.

Instead, find the answer on the answer sheet that summarizes or paraphrases the dialogue. Imagine a test on which the correct answers included exactly the same words as the questions. That might be too simple to answer for English learners at any level. Don't forget that test makers try to make their tests appropriately difficult and sometimes tricky.

Hint 5: Don't focus on sentence structures.

Instead, focus on only content words that are important for you to understand the contents and the flow of each talk. When you write or say something, correct structure is important for you to make yourself understood for your listeners or readers. However, for some listening selections, you might not have enough time to carefully analyze the structure in them. For instance, when you listen to a weather forecast such as "London will be partly cloudy with a high of 35 and a low of 30 degrees" the information you should listen for is just "London," "partly cloudy," "high of 35," and "low of 30." If you were interested in learning how to use this vocabulary, you could listen carefully to the full sentence and it would help you enhance your variety of expression. However, for TOEIC listening comprehension, just listening for content words is usually enough.

Hint 6: Don't try to translate the dialogues into your first language.

Instead, think of answering the questions as just a scanning task without any translation process. For the scanning task, each dialogue works as simply a source of information. What you have to do is to pick up the information piece that fits the question. Given that the structures of English and other languages differ, translation tasks need much more time than scanning does.

The TOEFL and the TOEIC are how learners are assessed outside the advanced classroom. In the classroom, assessment techniques used for beginning and intermediate students are also appropriate for advanced students. If learners are planning to take standardized tests like the TOEIC and TOEFL, they may benefit from practice using **responsive listening** and **information transfer questions**. Responsive listening asks the learner to listen to a question and choose from several answers, or listen to a conversation and answer questions about it. Information transfer questions are often based on a picture, as in the TOEIC. The learner hears a sentence, or sometimes a longer description, and chooses the picture that best describes what was heard.

One alternative form of assessment that works very well is a **portfolio** through which learners reflect on their progress. At an advanced level, learners are prepared to discuss their learning in sophisticated ways. A portfolio is a folder or binder that contains examples of learner work. The teacher makes it clear to the learners what kinds of assignments should go into the portfolio, but the learners are responsible for choosing the material they include. The purpose is for the learners to show what they can do. A listening portfolio would contain:

- a statement from the student that introduces the portfolio and tells why its contents were selected.
- samples of classroom work. This can be work specifically on listening or other work that includes listening.
- samples of outside-of-class work. In addition to expected "academic homework" assignments, this may include summaries of non-academic listening experiences such as watching movies or TV or listening to a conversation in English.
- a reflection on learning: self-evaluation of strengths and weaknesses, what was learned by doing the portfolio, what learning strategies the learner has used (see pages 65–68 for learning strategies).

7. Conclusion

In this chapter, we have explored the teaching of listening to advanced learners. We began by looking at three issues that are especially important to consider when teaching advanced learners: discourse, culture, and authenticity. We then extended our discussion of these issues by focusing on three important principles to consider when teaching at this level. Next, we examined a variety of task types and materials useful for teaching advanced learners. We then looked at how some of these tasks could be used in the classroom. Finally, we discussed standardized testing and alternative assessments for advanced learners.

Further readings

Brown, S. and J. Eisterhold. 2004. *Topics in Language and Culture for Teachers.* Ann Arbor, MI: University of Michigan Press.

This textbook for future teachers gives background in how language and culture are related. It also includes information on discourse.

Lynch, T. 2004. *Study Listening* 2nd ed. Cambridge, UK: Cambridge University Press.

This is an excellent example of an academic listening text.

McCarthy, M. and S. Walsh. 2003. Discourse in D. Nunan (ed.) *Practical English Language Teaching.* New York, NY: McGraw Hill ESL/ELT, 173–195.

This chapter presents the basics of how discourse is organized.

Rost, M. 2002. *Teaching and Researching Listening.* Harlow, UK: Longman/Pearson Education.

This book is a thorough discussion of listening and research. The section on teaching listening is particularly useful.

Helpful Web sites

TOEFL (www.ets.org/toefl/)

This is the official site for TOEFL. It has a comprehensive explanation of the changes made for the "new" TOEFL and listening practice activities for test-takers.

TOEIC (www.ets.org/toeic/)

This is the official site for TOEIC and has an overview of the test and test prep tools.

Dave's ESL café (www.eslcafe.com/)

This site, also mentioned in Chapter 3, is a great resource for teachers interested in using TV, movies, and music. You may find useful lesson ideas, worksheets, etc. in the Teacher Forums—video in the classroom section and in the Idea Cookbook video and music sections.

References

Brown, S. and L. Menasche. Defining Authenticity [updated 2005; cited Oct. 2005]. Available from www.as.ysu.edu/%7Eenglish/sbrown.html.

Craven, M. 2004. *Listening Extra*. Cambridge, UK: Cambridge University Press.

Freeman, D., K. Graves, and L. Lee. 2005. *Icon 3* New York, NY: McGraw-Hill.

Harsch, K. and K. Wolfe-Quintero. (2001). *Impact 3*. Hong Kong: Longman Asia ELT.

Hartmann, P. and L. Blass. 2000. *Quest 3 Listening and Speaking*. New York, NY: McGraw-Hill.

Helgesen, M., S. Brown, and T. Mandeville. 2004. *English Firsthand 2*. Hong Kong, PRC: Longman/Pearson Education Asia.

Kozyrev, J. 2002. *Talk it Over: Listening, Speaking and Pronunciation,* Boston, MA: Houghton Mifflin.

Lund, R.J. 1990. A Taxonomy for Teaching Second Language Listening. *Foreign Language Annals* 23:105-115.

Nunan, D. 2004. *Task-Based Language Teaching*. Cambridge, UK: Cambridge University Press.

Richards, J.C. 1985. *The Context of Language Teaching*. Cambridge, UK: Cambridge University Press.

Sadow, C. and E. Sather. 1998. *On the Air: Listening to Radio Talk*. Cambridge, UK: Cambridge University Press.

Soukhanov, A.H. ed. 1999. *Encarta World English Dictionary*. New York, NY: St. Martin's Press.

Chapter **Five**

Key issues in teaching listening

At the end of the chapter, you should be able to:

Goals

✔ **explain** the idea of "listening as a social activity."

✔ **discuss** uses of technology in teaching listening including video and the Internet.

✔ **identify** steps learners can use to develop autonomy.

✔ **understand** extensive listening and suggest ways to implement it.

✔ **identify** principles of learning styles and multiple intelligences and how they relate to learning to listen.

✔ **evaluate** a series of "top five" lists for listening teachers and develop your own list.

1. Introduction

In this chapter, we will consider several key issues that teachers and learners often need to deal with when teaching listening skills. We'll begin by making the point that listening is often a social activity. As such, listening happens constantly, even in classes dedicated to the other language skills. We will then look at technology, specifically the use of video and of the Internet for helping learners develop listening skills. Next, we will focus on **extensive listening** and self-study/learner-**autonomy** issues. We will then consider the learning styles and preferences of students and the range of intelligences that exist. Finally, we will share a series of experts' "top five things listening teachers need to remember" and encourage readers to write their own.

2. Listening as a social activity

The Greek philosopher Epictetus said, "We have two ears and one mouth so that we can listen twice as much as we speak."

In addition to giving some pretty good advice, Epictetus points out an important fact: listening happens between people. A vast majority of the time that we are speaking, we are listening as well. In this book, we've been focusing on listening, but teachers need to recognize and remember that most classroom activities involve more than one skill. Almost every speaking activity is at least 50 percent a listening activity. When students read, they are often talking to each other—and themselves—about the text. This is often true of writing activities as well. It is useful to think of this as a resource. How can we maximize the effectiveness of listening that happens outside of the specific listening tasks? Do we, for example, set up speaking tasks that require learners to pay attention and respond to what their partners say? Do we give classroom instructions in English, thus providing extra practice, or do we speak in the learners' native language? If we feel bilingual instructions are necessary, do we give the instructions in English first to give learners a chance to try to understand the meaning before we give them in the easier native tongue?

An important aspect of getting the message as we listen is being able to see our partner's facial expressions and body language. When we talk to someone, we can see (or at least guess at) their age, gender, and social circumstances (often based, for example, on how they are dressed). Most listening textbooks rely completely on audio, and these kinds of clues are missing when students listen without seeing. We'll look at the issue of using images as well as audio in the next section, but first let's look at some tips on how we can teach learners to listen "socially."

- Put the students in social situations. Let them speak to each other. Remember, your students are learning English to communicate, so let them. Pair work and group work have become common parts of English language teaching, but some teachers are still reluctant to use them too much.
- Teach active listening. Active listening means responding to the person you're talking to, keeping the conversation going by asking questions, and making comments. Sometimes it means just showing interest, and sometimes it means stopping the other person to make sure you're understanding him or her. Sometimes a poster on the wall is enough to encourage active listening. Teach a few **back channeling** phrases like *Really?, I don't think I understand you,* and *Could you say that again?* As students work in pairs or small groups, the teacher can monitor their use of these phrases and point them out on the poster if learners are forgetting to use them.
- Teach culturally appropriate listening. We've noted that cultures differ on how they give feedback to the people they're listening to. We tend to use our native culture when first speaking a second or foreign language. Learners first need to be made aware of what they do in their native language and how, if at all, it differs from the language they're learning. Observation tasks are a good way to do this. In a foreign language situation, this may mean watching TV or movies to try to figure out important signals people give each other while speaking. As we'll see, the sound can be turned off and learners can focus on body language like nodding the head or leaning closer to the speaker. In a second language situation, it may mean sending the students to a public place like a park or shopping mall to observe people having conversations.
- Since listening has a social dimension, it is useful to remember that different people react differently in social situations. Some people are open and gregarious. Others are more reserved. One of the advantages of doing activities in pairs and small groups is it means more reticent speakers have a chance to speak. This topic leads to the question of shy students. In language class, like anywhere else, shy students are less comfortable. That will happen, but it is important to note the difference between shyness and fear. Nearly everyone feels uncomfortable speaking—especially a foreign language—if they are afraid of losing face in front of other people. In our own classes, we rarely call on people to answer in front of the whole class. It is usually much easier and less threatening to do an activity where they are speaking in front of only one to three partners.

3. Using technology in the listening classroom

Video

We're using "video" here as a general term for specially produced language-teaching packages, for recorded television and movies (fiction and documentary), as well as teacher-produced and learner-produced materials. Though they're very important issues, we're going to ignore questions about the legality of using recorded television programs and about whether viewing all or parts of movies in class constitutes "fair use" under copyright laws. Our readers are in several countries that have different laws. We strongly advise teachers to follow the policies laid out by their schools (and we strongly encourage schools to get good information about the copyright law).

Reflection

1. Have you used video in a language classroom, either as a teacher or as a student?

2. What was the purpose?

3. What did you find useful or enjoyable about using video?

4. Was there anything you didn't like?

Share your answers with a classmate or colleague.

The first question to ask is: *Is teaching with video teaching listening?* After all, the students can see most of the information needed to understand without listening. A colleague once used the analogy of driving a car while listening to the radio. If something happens on the road, you focus all your attention on the visual and ignore the audio. Similarly, he felt that the visual overrides the audio when students view a video. That may sometimes be true; however, for the most part, when watching a video, as in most real life situations, we get information from both our ears and our eyes. In fact, in real life, we also potentially get information from our nose, tongue, and fingers as well. We would expect video viewing to be easier because more than one sense is involved. Actually, particularly in news and documentaries (but also in fiction films with voice-over), what students hear and what they see might be two different things. Television news often presents the images that its producers think tell the story most clearly (and raise the most emotions in viewers). These images may or may not be connected exactly to what the reporter is saying on the audio. They may have to do with something that came earlier (a disaster, for example) or will come later (images of last year's summit meeting coupled with a report about the summit meeting to take place next week). So video can be more difficult as well as easier for learners to use, especially when there is a conflict between what people are seeing and what they are hearing.

1. Watch a newscast (in any language) and see how closely the audio and visual match. If possible, also watch newscasts in other languages to see if there are any cultural differences.

2. Video tape a segment of a newscast. First, watch it with the sound off. See what you understood. A day or so later, when the ideas are not fresh in your mind, listen to the newscast without looking at the pictures. Again, a day or two later, watch the video while listening. Notice how the sound and images interact, both on the screen and in your understanding.

3. If you have access to a video in a language you know somewhat, watch the video. As you watch, notice what you understand and which items you understand from the visuals, which you understand from the audio, and which you understand because of your background knowledge.

Share your answers with a classmate or colleague.

___

If video is usually more difficult than audio, why use it? It's motivating. Learners belong to a visual culture. In most cases, learners have grown up with TV and movies. Visual stimulation is part of their everyday lives. It is also more like real life. In daily communication we can see the situation, notice gestures, facial expressions, body language, physical proximity of speakers, and the like. Video can bring these elements into the classroom in ways audio recordings can't. This is especially useful in EFL situations because video can bring in other cultures. The class can work on cross-cultural differences in language use (apologies, requests, etc.) and in body language. Even a task as simple as watching and noticing physical things the students would or wouldn't do in their own cultures can be useful.

How do you use video? Basically any listening activity that can be done with audio (except ones, obviously, that ask the students to imagine what the speakers look like) can be, and probably has been, done with video. Unfortunately, many teachers have relied solely on "listen and fill in the blank" exercises and comprehension questions when using video. Here are several generic activities that make use of the audio and the visual of videos, first in sequence and then together. All of these activities use just one short scene of a couple of minutes.

- **Strip stories**. Prepare a handout with the events of the scene in scrambled order (it's best to cut the worksheet into strips with one sentence on each strip). As students listen with the picture off but the sound on (just hang a sheet of paper over the screen), they sequence the events. Show the scene again with the picture on.
- **Dialogue differences**. Prepare a worksheet with three short possible dialogues for each scene and give them to the students. Turn the sound off. Play the scene. Students guess what's going on. Play the scene again with the sound on. Students check their answers. For advanced classes, you don't need to prepare the dialogues. Just have them guess.
- **Silent viewing**. Turn the sound off. Guess what the characters are saying or feeling based on their body language. Then turn the sound on. Listen to see how the body language goes with what is said.
- **Predict the action**. Show a video segment. Stop at a critical point. Have learners discuss what they think will happen next. Then they look at the segment to see if they were right.
- **What do you want to know?** Play a very short section from a film the students have not seen or heard much about. Unusual scenes work best. Students watch the scene. Then alone or in pairs, they write questions they would like answered about the scene. You may want to have them predict answers to their own or another pair's questions.
- **Five Ws and an H**. Write *who, what, when, where, why, how* on the board. Tell them they will see a video scene twice. They need to come up with six questions, one for each question word. Have the students just watch the scene. The second time they watch, they can take notes. Then alone or in pairs, they write their questions. Then they work with another student or another pair. They ask their questions. The new partner(s) try to answer. (We learned this technique from Susan Stempleski.)

Figure 1 is one more generic activity, one that makes use of TV (or radio) advertisements. It's a **critical listening** activity in which learners not only have to listen but think about what's behind what they are hearing. It can be done in class, as homework, or as self-access (see "Self-study and learner autonomy," pages 136–140).

Advertisement Worksheet

1. What product (or service) is being sold? ____________________
2. Who is the buyer? (Who is the ad for?) ____________________
3. How do you know? ____________________
4. What words are used to attract the buyer? ____________________
5. What images are used to attract the buyer? ____________________
6. Would you buy the product? ☐ Yes ☐ No
7. Why or why not? ____________________

____

Figure 1: Critical listening activity

Of course, the use of video raises questions about subtitles, not all of which have clear answers. Should we show the subtitles? If so, should they be shown in English or in the learners' native language?

As a rule of thumb, the brain processes most quickly whatever is easiest to process. That means that if we show the video with native language subtitles, it is unlikely the learners really process much English. However, there might be times you want to do that.

For example, television and Hollywood movies are very difficult for learners. However, as we mentioned before, they are very motivating. Some learners like to watch a video segment either in their native language or in English with native-language subtitles so they understand the story. Then they watch it again without the subtitles to see how much they understood.

In the section on extensive listening (pages 141–142), we'll argue in favor of watching easy English movies with English subtitles as a way of encouraging simultaneous extensive listening and extensive reading–and giving the learners an enjoyable experience in English at the same time.

The Internet

Over the past few years, the Internet has become a useful and exciting tool for language teachers. Like any new tool, it is taking time to learn how to use it effectively. Some ESL/EFL sites are wonderful, reflecting a deep understanding of how students learn. Some others, while featuring the visually exciting surface that technology has to offer, are actually rather shallow. Writing about the current state of the Internet can be a challenging task, not least because the Internet itself has changed hundreds of times since you began reading this paragraph. For that reason, we won't attempt to give a complete guide to listening on the Internet. You are better off finding out what is currently available by going to a search engine such as Google and searching for

ESL EFL listening. Instead, we'll mention a few resource types and sites that we find useful. You may want to compare them with others you come across.

Sites designed for ESL/EFL students

One of the best known is Randall's ESL Cyber Listening Lab (www.esl-lab.com/), created by Randall Davis, a computer language lab coordinator and ESL teacher in Utah who formerly worked in Japan. This free site features over 150 streaming RealMedia files and associated activities, each with a three-part lesson task: pre-listening exercises, multiple-choice listening exercises which the students do while listening, and post-listening follow-ups. The questions can be checked automatically, and transcripts and other supporting materials are available.

Audio

Example 1

CD Track 19

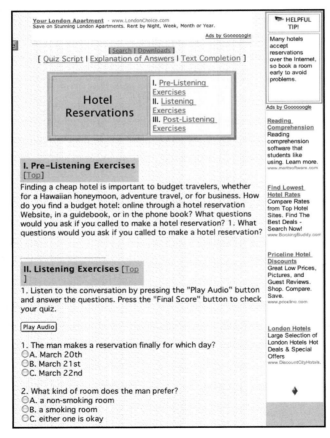

3. Why doesn't he want to reserve the suite?
○A. It doesn't have a nice view.
○B. It doesn't come with a sauna bath.
○C. It's too expensive.

4. Including tax, how much is the man's room?
○A. 80 dollars
○B. 88 dollars
○C. 96 dollars

5. How do you spell the man's name?
○A. Maxner
○B. Maexner
○C. Mexner

_____
[Final Score] [Reset]

Score = [_____]
Correct answers:

[   ]

2. Listen to the conversation again as you read the Quiz Script.

3. Review Explanation of Answers.

4. Do Text Completion Quiz.

III. Post-Listening Exercises
[Top]
1. Practice this conversation with a partner. Also, choose a city
you want to visit and use the Internet to find cheap, affordable
accomodations (hotels, youth hostels, etc.) that interest you.

[Quiz Script I Explanation of Answers I Text Completion]

Randall's ESL Cyber Listening Lab (www.esl-lab.com/hotel1/hotel1.htm)

All of the lessons on the ESL Cyber Listening Lab are categorized as
easy, medium, or difficult, so learners are able to find lessons that are at their
own levels. Example 1 is one of the site's "easy" level lessons.

Action

To notice the difference in levels on a recording by the same speakers and
a similar topic, go to www.esl-lab.com/checkin/checkinrd1.htm. Look at the
listening exercise. Listen to the hotel guest talking about a mix-up in
reservations.

Contrast it with the first segment. What aspects of the language (vocabulary,
delivery, structure) make it difficult? How do the questions make the task more
challenging?

Share your answers with a classmate or colleague.

Another useful site is Arlyn Freed's ESL/EFL listening resources (www.eslhome.com/esl/listen/). Created and maintained by a teacher with degrees in both multimedia and linguistics, this is a collection of links to various listening sites. A unique feature of the site is that it gives an overview of the advantages and disadvantages of the various sites listed. It also has a good list of content-based listening sites with authentic and semi-authentic recordings.

Podcasts

Podcasting is making audio files available on-line, usually in MP3 format. There are a variety of podcasts aimed at ESL and EFL learners. Most are run by individual teachers and range in topic from general language learning discussion/lessons and newscasts to those focused on specific issues like idioms or songs. A useful list of podcasts for learners is at: http://iteslj.org/links/ESL/Listening/Podcasts/.

Voice chat

Since the beginning of the Internet boom of the 1990s, "key pals" (Internet pen pals) have been popular with English students around the world. Recently, the introduction of Skype and other Internet telephone services have made voice chat possible. One site is www.mylanguageexchange.com/VoiceChat.asp. Students can find people who want to engage in voice chat. While we see these innovations as exciting, we also encourage teachers to make sure students know what kind of information they should and should not give out to strangers. A couple years ago, one of our students was in an Internet class where they were learning to post messages on an Internet bulletin board service. It was a fairly large class so the teacher didn't know what everyone was posting. As he moved around the classroom, one group of students covered up a monitor so he couldn't see. The teacher said, "I respect your privacy. You don't have to show me what you want to post. But keep in mind you are about to post that on the Internet where anyone can see it." It turns out the student had written, "I am a 20-year-old girl. I am very lonely because I have no lover." "Hmm," the teacher said, "That's going to get you lots of key pals." It turns out she had meant to say she had no "boyfriend." Students need to know that they shouldn't give out personal information. For many teachers and learners this will be obvious, but given the number of people who get hurt by Internet fraud, it is probably worth mentioning.

Content sites

Many teachers use the Internet as a way of providing non-fiction content to ESL and EFL classes. The challenge, of course, is finding sites that provide content that is comprehensible. For advanced learners, news sites like www.npr.org (National Public Radio), and www.cnn.com can be wonderful. The BBC offers a major resource of free materials at www.bbc.co.uk/worldservice/learningenglish/index.shtml for learners of all levels. You can often find useful materials at sites like www.yahooligans.com and www.kidsclick.org. Type your topic into the search box along with the word *audio*. Although these sites are designed for children, if you are looking for non-fiction material on topics such as culture, it is often available in a format that is not childish.

Music

In Chapter 2, we mentioned that music was useful for listening at the highest level, appreciation. Most students love music. It is, of course, easy to find on-line. Sites such as www.mtv.com and music.yahoo.com provide music videos in a variety of genres. The key is comprehensibility. Lyrics are often available at music-related sites. If they are not, you can find them by going to a search engine like google.com and typing the name of the song and the word *lyrics*.

Probably the most common task for songs is creating a cloze exercise. As we alluded to in Chapter 2, it has always struck us that this is a sad thing to do to a song. Music can be such a great source of pleasure, emotion, and thinking, that reducing them to "listen and catch the missing words" is really a lost chance. Here are a few possible tasks that don't require a lot of preparation time but can get at higher level processing.

- Listen to the song (with or without seeing the words). Draw a picture based on your image of the song. Explain your picture to a partner.
- Dictate about 10–15 key words from the song. Have students write each on a small piece of paper. Then they listen and put the words in order.
- Make copies of the lyrics. Cut them into strips (each with one or two lines). Students read the strips and try to put them in order. Then they listen and check or change the order. (If the song tells a story, you can just cut the verses apart.)
- Listen to a song that tells a story. With a partner, decide what happens next or what happened before. Tell your story to another group.
- Write five or more events from a song that tells a story on the board. Listen. Put the events in order.
- Listen with the lyrics. Talk about the meaning. Then sing.

In this section, we've looked at several different ways of using the technology of video and of the Internet. Like any tool, they can be used in many different ways. We find remembering that they are means to an end rather than the end itself is important. One of the real benefits of technology is that it makes it easier for learners to study on their own, which leads us to the topic of learner autonomy.

4. Self-study and learner autonomy

To really improve in a language, learners need to work on their own as well as in class. They need to take charge of their own learning, to develop autonomy. As teachers, we need to support this outside work with structures that guide the students. It's not enough just to say, "Go home and listen." We need to give them ideas (for one example, see pages 137–138). We can also provide a structure through a **listening center**, an area in a school with tape/CD/DVD players and computers where students can work on listening on their own.

Action

1. In your own experience as a teacher and/or language learner, what have you done to encourage your students or yourself to work on listening independently? List as many things as you can.

- _____ • _____ • _____

- _____ • _____ • _____

- _____ • _____ • _____

2. Use your imagination. What other things could you or the students do?

3. Now look at your list again. How many of these things would the students (or you) actually do if they were not required?

Share your answers with a classmate or colleague.

Thirty years ago, schools all had language laboratories. Most of the material designed for language laboratories was of the "listen and repeat" type. This was typical of practice activities associated with **ALM (the Audio-Lingual Method)**, a behavioristic theory of language learning that assumed language was simply a matter of habit formation and enough practice. While practice is a good thing, having the students simply repeat a sentence until it becomes automatic is not the best way to learn a language. Twenty years ago, schools were building new language laboratories in response to the then-new communicative approach. These labs allowed learners to talk to each other through microphones and headphones. We found they could talk and listen to each other without the technology. Rather than being the traditional "listen and repeat" practice rooms of the past, current language laboratories (often called language resource centers, self-access centers, or listening centers) are often more likely to be places where students can go to work on their language by themselves or with a friend.

If there are computers, students can use the resources we discussed in the previous section on technology. If there are DVD players, they can watch movies. Some centers have textbooks that are not used in classes. Learners can check these books out and use the accompanying audio programs. Learners, in addition to getting the book and audio, get an overhead transparency (a page-sized piece of plastic) and a pen with water-soluble ink (an overhead projector pen). They put the plastic over the textbook page and mark their answers. When they're done, the plastic sheet can be easily cleaned.

Recently, many ESL and EFL textbooks have started including student self-study CDs. These can, of course, be excellent resources for autonomous learning. Unfortunately, many students don't realize the many options they have for practicing with the CD. Figure 3 shows 12 self-study practice ideas. You'll notice that many of them fit in with the idea of going back and looking at form (**FonF**) after students have worked on the meaning of the text. If your textbook has a student practice CD but doesn't give specific tasks or ways to practice, we suggest you copy this list and give it to the students.

Using the CD on your own

Your progress in English depends on your effort. Practice both in and outside of class. Try to practice on your own between classes. If you can review just before a lesson, you'll be ready to make the most of the class.

Listening tasks
After you've done the listening in class, review it several times. Decide how you want to review:

Just listen. After you have listened in class, go back and listen a few more times. Just listen and see how much you understand. Don't worry about understanding everything. Think about what you DO understand.

The movie in your mind. Close your eyes as you listen. Imagine the people and their conversations the same way you imagine scenes as you read a book. **HINT:** If you have a portable CD player and go to work or school by train or bus, this is an easy way to review. After reviewing the lesson you have just studied, go back to past lessons. Listen to them again.

✓ *Check the answers again.* Look at the listening pages of your book. Try to notice the answers as they are spoken on the CD. You may want to touch the answers in your book as you hear them.

Figure 2: Listening self-study tasks   (continued)

? How did I know that? Look at the listening pages of your book. As you listen, notice the correct answers. How did you know? What words gave you the information? **HINT:** This is a good activity to do with a partner. Share your information. Did you both use the same hints?

Focus on form. Think about the grammar or language function of the lesson. Then listen to the CD. How many times can you find those forms (patterns) in the recording? If you have a copy of the script, underline the key patterns as you hear them.

How much do you remember? Look at the answers in your book. What else do you remember about what you heard? Where were the people? What information did they mention? Can you remember some words they used? See how much you can remember. Then listen to check.

Back to the beginning. Once you get one third or halfway through the book, go back to Unit 1 or 2. Most students are surprised—and happy—to see how much easier it is now.

Textbook conversations: just listen. Close your book. Listen to the conversation. How much did you understand?

Pronunciation focus #1: Listen and say. Listen to the conversation. Stop the CD after each sentence. Repeat the sentences. Try to match the rhythm and stress of the sentence. **HINT:** It's a good idea to repeat it silently before you say it out loud. This helps you focus on pronunciation.

Pronunciation focus #2: Say, then listen. Look at each line. Think about the pronunciation, especially the stress and rhythm. Say it. Then play that line on the CD. Compare your own pronunciation.

Work on speed. Play the conversation. Try to read it out loud at the same time you listen. Work on speed and on matching the stress. **HINT:** If you repeat silently, you will probably be able to focus on your pronunciation more easily. Move your mouth, tongue, etc. Just don't make sounds.

Write it right. Listen to the dialogue two or three times. Then put your book away. Try to write the dialogue. Then listen again. Compare what you wrote with the recording. Remember, there are many ways to say anything in English. Some of the words you wrote may be different. If you made mistakes with grammar, correct them. **HINT:** Try this with a partner.

The CD can help you practice and learn. But, of course, no one can do it for you. It's up to you. **You can do it!**

Figure 2: Adapted from *English Firsthand 1 Teacher's Manual* (Helgesen, Brown, and Mandeville, 2004, pp. CO3–CO4)

Another simple way to give students access to extra listening is to use radio news broadcasts with intermediate and advanced learners. We've noted the radio-based sources like NPR on the Internet, but many countries receive the BBC, the Voice of America, and/or the United States Armed Forces Radio. Radio news is something learners seem to like, so it's motivating. They have schemata for it, because they have heard or can hear the same story in their native languages. The broadcasts are short (usually about three to five minutes) and there are usually at least three stories in each broadcast, so if they can't understand one, they can always try the next. Example 1 is a worksheet for listening to the radio news in a self-access environment. This is for an intermediate class studying in the United States, preparing to enter an American university (Smith 2005).

Example 1

NPR News

1. Listen to the news. Put the stories in the correct order. Write 1–4.
2. Listen to the news stories again. Each time you hear one of the words or phrases from the following vocabulary list, put an 'x' in the column of the story that you heard it in.
3. Listen one more time and take notes on the details of one item. Then write a summary of that item.

	Terry Schiavo	Red Lake High School shooting	Pres. Bush/ Vicente Fox/ Paul Martin meeting	Explosion in Texas City, TX
Principal				
Supreme Court				
oil refinery				
immigration reform				
guest worker				
feeding tube				
opened fire				
brain damage				
Summit				
irreversible				

As you can see, the worksheet on page 139 is quite easy for a teacher to produce, and you can make the grid as long or short as necessary. Notice also that this framework could be used with any number of news stories. The teacher would write a title for each story and a list of vocabulary words. It could be a weekly assignment. Or the grid could be left completely blank, and learners could use the blank grids to write the titles of the stories they heard and the vocabulary they picked up for each story. If writing skills were not a priority, the teacher could eliminate the third task.

Self-access materials need to be simple, because the teacher won't be around to answer questions. For that reason, simple tasks that don't require a lot of instructions are best. It's also a good idea to use frames, the same sorts of worksheets each time (like grids) so that students instantly know what they're doing because they've done it before.

Teachers may also want a way to keep track of what learners are doing outside of class. This may be as simple as asking learners to sign in when they use the self-access center. Or it may involve asking learners to keep a journal or learning log. A journal could just be a simple diary of what they did outside of class to work on their English. Example 2 is one kind of learning log.

Example 2

It's up to you **LearningLog.**

Name: _____   Student number: _____

Please try to do (at least) one out-of-class listening practice activity each week. Write: when you did it, what you did, and your feelings/ideas about it.

When:	**What you did:**	**Feeling/idea:**
(Example)		
9/10	Went to karaoke with my friends. Sang 3 songs in English: Yesterday, Top of the world, and one more (forgot the name)	This was really fun. I'll do this again.

Extensive listening

Reading teachers recognize the importance of "extensive reading"–reading a lot of easy material, often for pleasure, with a minimal task or no task at all. It is useful for increasing vocabulary, motivation, grammar skills, and even listening ability (Day and Bamford, 1998). And, since this is something learners can do on their own, it builds autonomy. Extensive reading is the counter-balance to building academic reading skills (skimming, scanning, identifying main ideas, etc.) and is recognized as an essential part of any reading program. Yet until recently there has been little interest or research into extensive listening. Indeed, a summer 2005 Google search for "extensive reading" produced over 144,000 hits. A search for "extensive listening" produced fewer than 9,000. Like its reading counterpart, extensive listening means learners listen to large amounts of easy material.

One very easy way of working on extensive listening is to combine it with extensive reading. Many publishers have "graded readers" designed for second or foreign language learners. They are graded so learners can find books that they can easily understand and enjoy. Many of the readers come with CDs or tapes on which the stories are professionally read or acted. One of the ways children learn to read is when their parents or teachers read stories to them. Having students read the story and listen along with the recording serves the same function. They can also read the story first, then listen without the book to see how much they understand. The reading step provides the schema for understanding. Other learners prefer to listen first, then go back and read to check how much they understood. Allowing students to make choices is important for both learner autonomy and for dealing with different learning styles, a topic we'll explore in the next section of this chapter.

In an earlier section, we talked about using video. Most students love Hollywood movies. Unfortunately, most blockbusters, as popular as they are, are at a level that makes them too difficult for extensive listening or, more precisely, extensive viewing. An exception is animation. Films from studios such as Pixar (*Finding Nemo, Toy Story*), Dreamworks (*Shrek, Madagascar*), Disney (*The Incredibles, Beauty and the Beast, Lion King*), and Studio Ghibli (*Spirited Away, My Neighbor Totoro,* and *Howl's Moving Castle*) are often ideal because they are written at a level that is simple enough for children as well as language learners to understand. At the same time, the stories themselves are entertaining for adults and do not feel condescending or childish. At the university where one of the authors of this book teaches, we often show these during lunch hour. Learners are encouraged to bring their lunch and watch the film, which is projected onto a large screen. To provide extra support for understanding, we play the films on DVD with the English subtitles visible. It usually takes two or three lunch periods to view an entire film. The sessions are voluntary and the room is usually full of eager students. This means, of course, that learners are volunteering to listen to, read, and enjoy English for an extra hour or two each time we show a film.

Some teachers question making the subtitles visible. As we said earlier, we find it is useful for comprehension. Without them the film would be too difficult. While we don't suggest providing subtitles or a script with most intensive listening tasks, we find that they are useful for extensive listening, especially when we are asking learners to listen for long periods of time. It is building listening and reading skills at the same time.

News sites on the Internet provide another way for students to listen as they read scripts. We mentioned the BBC earlier. Their site has the "authentic" broadcasts but provides extra support such as scripts with key vocabulary explained. Of course, not all learners want or need the tapescripts. They are there as a tool for teachers and students who choose to use them. And, like any tool, there are many different ways to use them: simultaneous listening and reading, reading as a preview to listening, listening before reading to check, reading only the key vocabulary, etc. The Voice of America offers broadcasts in English. They also feature articles in "special English," which are simple, highly articulated broadcasts. Some would argue that such carefully enunciated language is not authentic, but as we pointed out in Chapter 4 (pages 101–103), "authentic" is not a simple term. We need to ask "authentic for whom?" If your students find these useful, then maybe they are good for those learners.

5. Dealing with learning styles, preferences, and multiple intelligences

In recent years, there has been an upsurge of interest in and understanding of the ways people learn. Some researchers look at sensory preferences, identifying people as primarily visual, auditory, tactile, or kinesthetic (Kinsella, 1995). Others have looked at variables such as how learners prefer to analyze information, deal with concrete items like videos and recordings, interact with each other and/or with an "authority figure" like a teacher or a textbook (Nunan, 2004).

Yet another way of looking at learning is to consider the **multiple intelligences (MI)** of learners, that is, the "theory of intelligence that characterizes human intelligences as having multiple dimensions that must be acknowledged and developed in education" (Richards and Schmidt, 2003, p. 346).

While all of these systems are different, they are similar in that they acknowledge that all learners do not process and learn things in the same way. They all speak to the fact that, as teachers, we need to provide a rich environment of varied experiences.

Based on the work of Howard Gardner (1999) and others, MI theory usually identifies eight specific intelligences: verbal-linguistic, logical-mathematical, visual-spatial, bodily-kinesthetic, musical-rhythmic, intrapersonal, interpersonal, and naturalistic.

It is important to understand that it is not a matter of figuring out which one each student is and teaching them in that way. As Pugliese puts it, "MI is not about labeling people" (2005, p. 5). Everyone has all the intelligences, but to different degrees. And our success in areas related to a given intelligence may vary depending on the activities we are doing. Regardless of the system of looking at preferences or intelligences, the key is to provide a range of experiences so everyone gets some work in their areas of strength as well as input that can strengthen their weaker areas.

The eight basic intelligences, plus activities that can be used with listening to work with this area of strength, are in Figure 4 on pages 144–145.

- **Verbal-linguistic intelligence (word smart).** This is an intelligence we don't need to worry about since listening to language is already in the "verbal-linguistic" area. Listening activities work on it, as do tasks involving vocabulary, storytelling (and listening), and the like. The acquisition-friendly Focus on Form activities described in Chapter 3, which encourage scanning scripts to find certain structures, appeal to these learners.

- **Logical-mathematical intelligence (logic smart).** This is the area that education has traditionally valued and tested. Many of the activities in textbooks work with this intelligence, such as answering questions, classifying and categorizing, sequencing, and outlining. Of course, knowing the task before listening is essential.

- **Visual-spatial intelligence (picture smart).** This is related to visual images. Many textbooks are well-illustrated and appeal to learners strong in this area. If you are making your own material, remember that illustrations are not just for decoration. They are important for helping visual learners learn. Adding clip-art illustrations, charts, and graphs can make a big difference. Asking learners to do activities in which they imagine visual images and draw pictures can be useful, too.

- **Bodily-kinesthetic intelligence (body smart).** People strong in this area learn by doing: movement, gesture, and hands-on learning are essential. In the classroom, TPR (Total Physical Response) activities, as well as role play and other chances to move around the classroom, are important. Activities that include drawing are good, too. The acquisition-friendly activities such as working with scripts for role play and dialogue practice work with this intelligence. In many ways, bodily-kinesthetic learners have traditionally not been highly valued in school (except those who excel at sports) because they need to move around. Just sitting still can be a challenge. If we give these learners physical things to do in response to listening, we are helping them channel energy into their strengths.

- **Musical-rhythmic intelligence (music smart).** Of course this involves music, but it goes beyond that to include an awareness of tone, rhythm, pitch, and the human voice. Listening activities for which students are given a script and have to mark accents or patterns of pausing can build on this skill. Clapping rhythms and stress patterns can increase these learners' awareness. (Clapping, of course, appeals to kinesthetic learners as well. Many tasks cross over categories.)

Figure 4   (continued)

- **Intrapersonal intelligence (self smart).** These learners like to know their own thinking and feeling. The self-assessment ideas mentioned in Chapter 3 appeal to learners with high levels of intrapersonal intelligence. At times, you'll notice learners who prefer doing activities alone rather than in pairs or groups. They may be intrapersonal learners. Giving the class the choice of working alone or with a partner is one way to accommodate these students. Giving everyone a minute or two to think about a task before they listen and to think about their answers after they listen is a good idea, too.

- **Interpersonal intelligence (people smart).** These people work very well with others. We already mentioned that listening is usually a social activity—we listen as we interact with other people. Having the class do activities like warm-ups, peer-checking, and discussion will help these learners.

- **Naturalistic intelligence (environment smart).** We often think of these learners as focused on nature, but the environment includes their classroom surrounding as well. Naturalistic learners are often good at recognition, classification, and organization activities. These activities can be built into listening.

Figure 3: Eight multiple intelligences

This brief look at MI and listening reinforces a theme we have stressed throughout this book: variety. The variety of experiences, tasks, and listening types leads to more and deeper understanding.

Reflection

1. While reading the list of intelligences, do some of them "sound like you"? If they did, were the activities suggested the kind of things you like to do when you study or when you teach?

2. Did any of the intelligence types sound very different than your personal skills and talents? Did the activities suggested seem like things you wouldn't have thought of? If so, is it possible that they represent an area you usually don't deal with? Would that be reason enough to try them?

3. Can you think of people you know who seem to fit each category? Why do you think so?

Share your answers with a classmate or colleague.

6. Top five lists of ideas for listening teachers

In writing this book, we had to set priorities and make decisions. We could not present everything there is to know about listening. We had to decide what was the most important. As such, it was a process like what every teacher faces day-to-day in his or her classroom. What is important? What will I focus on?

Action

Think about what you have learned from this book. Also, reflect on your own experience as a learner (of language and everything else). If you have experience as a teacher, think about that, too.

What are five things important for you to remember when you are teaching listening? Write them.

- _____
- _____
- _____
- _____
- _____

Share your list with a classmate or colleague.

We invited a series of listening experts to give us a very short list of five items they believe are essential for listening teachers to remember. What follows are lists by several listening experts. As we were compiling these lists, we noticed two things in particular.

First, the lists are incredibly varied. Even though all of the experts are very aware of current research, teaching methodologies, and classroom practices, there was little agreement in the lists. We doubt there is anything on any of the lists that the other researchers and writers would disagree with, but it was clear that everyone had different priorities. We believe this speaks to the complexity of teaching listening—and of teaching in general. Different learners learn differently. Teaching situations and goals vary. Because teaching is so complex, requiring us as teachers to keep many variables in mind, any group of people will identify different aspects as priorities. We believe all the ideas listed are important. It is up to us all as teachers to decide which we will focus on in a given class. Exercises such as coming up with a "Top 5" list are one way to achieve focus.

We also noted the balance of theory and practice. Everyone mentioned ideas informed by theory (top-down vs. bottom-up processing, facilitating acquisition, strategy work, etc.). But all the lists were also tempered by classroom and real-life experience. Too often, theory and practice are presented as opposite ends of a continuum. These lists suggest the opposite. Both are useful and important aspects of the same reality. Theory informs classroom practice which, in turn, informs theory. This is a useful cycle.

As you read the lists, think about your own priorities and what you consider important. You might want to note those ideas that are new to you or that you want to try in your own classroom, now or in the future.

Five things listening teachers need to remember
by David Nunan

Link classroom tasks to real-life tasks.
Learners should be shown how classroom tasks will help them achieve effective listening goals in the world outside the classroom.

Provide a wide range of listening input.
Learners need opportunities to process a wide range of listening input that ranges from authentic to simulated texts.

Teach listening strategies.
Learners who are aware of a range of strategies, and who are able to match their strategies to their listening purposes, will be better listeners and better learners.

Encourage learners to practice their listening skills out of class.
With developments in technology and media, listening material is now readily accessible. While class time spent on listening is important, it is not sufficient for developing high-level skills in the language.

Encourage learners to reflect on their learning.
Learners who reflect on how well they are doing, and are able to self-monitor and self-evaluate, will be better learners and more effective listeners.

David Nunan is the editor of the *Practical English Language Teaching* series. He is also the author of numerous articles and books including *Listen In* (Thomson Heinle) and *Task-Based Language Learning* (Cambridge University Press).

All of David Nunan's points build on things we have emphasized in this book. His final point, "encourage learners to reflect on their learning," speaks to helping students become independent and self-sufficient. The respected

ELT educator Earl Stevick is famous for saying, "Teach. Then test. Then get out of the way." Our job is to help learners develop skills, in this case listening skills, so they no longer need us. We are helping them become independent.

Five listening tips
by Jack Richards

Distinguish teaching from testing.
When you teach listening, assume that students need to develop skills and strategies they don't already have. Teaching means preparing students for listening tasks and giving guided practice in listening. Testing means asking them to demonstrate how well they can listen. Don't confuse the two.

Use pre-listening, while-listening, and post-listening activities appropriately.
Don't expect students to do all the work while they listen. Use both the pre-listening and post-listening phases to focus and review students' efforts and to support a cycle of while-listening activities.

Don't assume all listening should be based on authentic materials.
Students can benefit both from listening to prepared texts as well as authentic texts. The former are designed to provide graded and controlled input, the latter to provide unsimplified input. Both can support the development of listening skills.

Use listening both to develop comprehension and to facilitate acquisition.
Use listening texts in two ways: first, as a way of developing comprehension, and second, to facilitate language learning by going back to texts and identifying how language is used in the text.

Provide examples of English as an international language.
Remind students that they will need to understand English as spoken both by native speakers (with many different accents) as well as non-native speakers. Try to expose students to samples of both kinds of English.

Jack Richards is the author of the best-selling *Interchange* series (Cambridge) and *Listening Tactics* (Oxford) as well as many other books for teacher development.

Jack Richards' comments provide useful examples of theory and practice informing each other. Surprisingly, until recently there was a lot of resistance in some quarters to having non-native speakers on ELT recordings. Comments to publishers from reviewers and focus groups included rather provincial ideas (...*but they are studying American English*–or British, or

Australian, etc.) and some that ignored reality (*I don't want my students to hear "foreign" accents.*). Students will, of course, hear non-native accents in any English class. In the modern world, non-native speakers using English are as likely to be speaking with other non-natives as they are to be speaking to a native speaker. They need practice with that. And, from Australia to the UK to the USA and Canada, most English-speaking cultures are ethnically diverse. Even in an entirely English-speaking environment, the need to be able to understand speakers with different accents is important.

Five useful principles for teaching listening
by Michael Rost

Find "the right stuff."
Help your students find the kind of input—songs, movies, TV dramas, game shows, simplified stories, real interviews, live anecdotes—that make them *want* to listen in the second language. Sustaining motivation is the key to progress in listening.

Uncover the spoken language.
Coach your students in perceiving the "grammar" of conversational speech—its rhythms, timing, and pauses, and its assimilation and reduction patterns. Hearing accurately is the basis of building confidence in listening.

Focus on interpersonal listening.
Teach strategies for listening in live conversations—asking clarification questions, giving ongoing feedback and confirmation, making short comments to support the speaker, redirecting the topic. Most students want to become active listeners in the second language, and welcome strategy instruction and feedback.

Encourage interpretation.
Remember that teaching listening is about building expectations and developing interpretations, not finding correct answers. Design tasks that encourage predicting, guessing, analyzing, and giving personal responses.

Work on memory.
Experiment with recall techniques such as reconstructing, shadowing, and paraphrasing in the second language. Most of our students appreciate short-term memory training, even if it's hard work!

Michael Rost is author of *Teaching and Researching Listening* (Longman) and is series editor of *Impact Listening* (Longman).

Michael Rost stresses many of the personal elements involved in learning to listen, from noting learner interests to making use of clarification, feedback, and memory strategies. His comment, *encourage interpretation*, is very important. Improving listening ability is an ongoing process. Getting the "correct" answers on today's lesson is far less important than the overall skills that learners develop gradually.

Listening – Top Five
by John Flowerdew and Lindsay Miller

Give students practice in both bottom-up and top-down processing.
Bottom-up processing means building understanding by combining the smallest units of meaning into larger units. Top-down listening means getting the general gist and using background knowledge to fill in the gaps. Both are important in developing listening skills.

Provide opportunities for individualization in listening.
Learners naturally adopt different strategies to listening (e.g., some may prefer bottom-up or top-down approaches). Teachers need to provide opportunities for individuals to apply different strategies. Teachers may also indicate to students new strategies that they may not be using (e.g., focusing on main points, listening for key words, using inferential strategies, note-taking, etc.).

Focus on the cross-cultural dimension of listening.
Listening texts may contain cultural references which teachers can exploit with their students. Texts may contain references to types of food, work practices, historical allusions, beliefs and values, etc. with which students may not be familiar. These may be exploited for discussion activities in which students' own cultural practices are contrasted with those found in the listening text.

Contextualize listening.
Listening does not take place in a vacuum. Students will bring varying degrees of background knowledge to their listening. Teachers need to take account of this. In addition, other activities may accompany listening (e.g., taking notes, looking at visual images, or reading a related handout). This is more closely related to real-life listening and, in fact, may make the process easier.

Encourage students to adopt a critical perspective.
Language learning materials are often trivial in terms of content and activities. By encouraging students to adopt a critical attitude towards what they are hearing, teachers can help them engage more with the text, and this can prompt meaningful discussion. For example, in a listening text about

---

unemployment, students can be encouraged to discuss various policies which might alleviate this problem.

Flowerdew and Miller are well-known in ELT listening circles and are authors of *Second Language Listening: Theory and Practice*.

Lindsay Miller and John Flowerdew point out that listening materials can be trivial. We believe this raises an important issue. It is fairly easy to "entertain" a class with fun lessons. But in doing so, it is often the teacher or the book that is the center of attention. The "teacher as entertainer" often leaves the learners in the passive role of audience. It is far more important and useful to engage the learners in ways that respect and make use of their ideas.

Five things to do to teach listening
by Tony Lynch

Make your listening tasks realistic.
Base the tasks you create for learners on what *you* have understood of the listening text on first hearing. When devising tasks, it is very easy to get into the habit of allowing yourself to replay an interesting text several times—and even to make a transcript—before you decide on questions and activities for the class. Put yourself in their position; work from once-only hearing, not multiple hearings, and work from the spoken word, not a transcript.

Identify the problems in a listening text.
Don't assume you can predict what will actually cause your students problems as they listen. If possible, try listening tasks out before you use them in class. Lots of different things can be a source of difficulty (syntax, vocabulary, phonology, context, intended audience, etc.). In class, make sure you spend time not only on simply checking answers, but also on discovering why students got those answers wrong.

Integrate listening with the other skills.
It may be convenient to label a teaching session as "listening," but we rarely do nothing but listen. Look for ways of linking a listening text with similar input (reading, video) and with related output activities of speaking and writing. Listening doesn't have to be the stereotypical one-way activity with a taped source; conversation is the obvious example of listening and speaking in tandem.

Get the students to ask the questions.

There are lots of reasons for asking the learners to set their own questions sometimes. Here are four: (1) the importance of learner involvement in the learning process; (2) the value of questions that reflect a *learner's* understanding of a listening text, as opposed to that of the teacher or materials writer; (3) the opportunity this technique offers for insight into individuals' misunderstandings; (4) not least, the enjoyment that learners get from it.

Learn another language.

This may seem slightly odd. But I recommend it as a natural way of reminding yourself what it feels like not to understand very much in a foreign language. This is something we can easily forget, if we have reached an advanced level in the language we teach, or may never have known, if we teach our native language. My current experiences in an elementary Spanish class—and the comments I hear from my classmates—are giving me ideas for listening tasks in my English classes and helping me to appreciate my own students' achievements in listening.

Tony Lynch is a Senior Lecturer at the Institute for Applied Language Studies, University of Edinburgh, Scotland. Among his books are *Listening* (with Anne Anderson, Oxford University Press 1988) and a redesigned second edition of *Study Listening* (Cambridge University Press 2004). Tony's recent research has focused on second language task recycling, EAP learner autonomy, and issues of identity in second language learning. He can be contacted at A.J.Lynch@ed.ac.uk.

Tony Lynch comments that his suggestion to learn another language may seem odd. We don't think so. You may have noticed that many of the anecdotes we've used throughout this book, from the confused conversation at the Vatican in Rome to the Gimpo Airport tape, are based on things that the authors have experienced living abroad and traveling. If there seem to be many references to Japan in this book, it is because one of the authors lived in Japan for over 10 years, and the other has been there for nearly 25 years. Our own experiences with learning a language and dealing with the accompanying frustrations and successes inform our teaching. Learning another language, whether you live abroad or not, is an important way to understand the reality of the process from a student's perspective.

Our own top five
by Steve Brown and Marc Helgesen

Provide task variety and develop task awareness.
Learners need to listen for a wide range of purposes. They need to be aware of their purpose.

Ensure text variety.
In addition to different tasks, learners need lots of different samples to listen to: conversations, lectures, announcements, advertisements, songs, and more. In "real life," we listen to lots of different things. We should in the classroom, too.

Focus on meaning, then go back and do acquisition work.
Listening almost always starts from meaning. Once we have covered that, it is a good idea at times to go back and have students focus on the forms that convey that meaning.

Do a warm-up for schema activation.
Pre-listening warm-ups aren't just add-ons. They are an important way to get listeners to think about the topic and what they already know. They are "thinking in the right direction."

Practice, practice, practice.
There's an old joke about a traveler in New York looking for Carnegie Hall, a famous concert hall. He asks someone on the street, "How do I get to Carnegie Hall?" The stranger replied, "Practice, practice, practice!" The same can be said for listening. All of the things we have talked about— task awareness, strategies, schema activation, etc.—are important but, ultimately, you learn to listen by listening. It takes a lot of practice.

When we wrote the above "Practice, practice, practice" idea, we were thinking of students. We believe, however, that it applies to us teachers as well. One of our own teachers and mentors, John Fanselow, is known for encouraging teachers to "break the rules." By noticing what we do and then "trying the opposite," we learn what will happen when we do things differently–or at least what happened that time we did something differently. But we also learn about the way we usually do things. So, if you usually do listening at the beginning of class, try it in the middle or at the end. If students usually work alone, have them work in groups. If you usually control the tape or CD player, put the students in charge. If you usually dictate to them, have them dictate to you or each other. Experimentation leads to learning. So, we encourage you to experiment with the ideas we have presented in this book.

If you like an idea, try it. See how it really works in your classroom. Then try the opposite. See what happens then. If you don't like an idea, try it in both its regular and opposite form. Again, you are guaranteed to learn something from it.

Reflection

1. As you read people's "top five" lists, were there any ideas that surprised you?

2. Now that you have read other people's lists, are there any changes you would like to make to your own top five list (page 146)?

7. Conclusion

In this chapter, we began by pointing out that listening is usually a social activity. As we listen, we are interacting with others. We then looked at technology in teaching listening, in particular video and the Internet. We then turned to self-study and autonomy issues. We also considered extensive listening. We looked at the ways learners process information by considering learning styles/preferences and multiple intelligences.

We ended the chapter, and the book, by inviting several listening experts to identify their "top five" ideas that listening teachers should remember. We hope those ideas, and the other ideas in this book, are useful to you and that you are now more effective at helping your students become better listeners.

Further readings

Benson, P. (2003). Learner Autonomy in the Classroom. In D. Nunan, ed. *Practical English Language Teaching*. New York, NY: McGraw-Hill.

Stempleski, S. (2002). Video in the ELT Classroom: The Role of the Teacher. In J.C. Richards and W.A. Renandya, eds. *Methodology in Language Teaching: An Anthology of Current Practice*. Cambridge, UK: Cambridge University Press. 364–367.

Helpful Web sites

Sites for ESL/EFL students with listening activities

Arlyn Freed's ESL/EFL listening resources. (www.eslhome.com/esl/listen/)

Links to various listening sites including Ms. Freed's evaluations of the sites. No advertisements.

The Bob and Rob Show (http://englishcaster.com/bobrob/)

A lively, easy to understand conversational English lesson by two teachers, one American and one British.

Breaking News English (www.breakingnewsenglish.com/index.html)

Daily news stories. Each is recorded at two levels, elementary and intermediate.

Internet ESL Journal–Podcast List (http://iteslj.org/links/ESL/Listening/Podcasts/)

A list of various podcasts for ESL/EFL learners, including lessons on banking, idioms, and English phrases.

Randall's ESL Cyber Listening Lab (www.esl-lab.com/)

A large number of listening exercises, divided into easy, medium, and difficult levels.

Sites for native speakers (and others) with or without ESL/EFL adaptations

BBC Radio Service (www.bbc.co.uk/worldservice/learningenglish/index.shtml)

A classic site for English teachers around the world. The site includes English lessons on current news, grammar, and vocabulary. Also includes a chat room.

Cable News Network (www.cnn.com)

The number one television news station in the world has a Web site with a free video feed of breaking news stories and newspaper-like articles.

Kidsclick (www.kidsclick.org)

This site is a project of the Ramapo Catskill Library System. It is a search engine designed for children by librarians. This site is especially good for teachers with young learners since it has strong filters that make sure adult sites do not appear on the screen.

National Public Radio (www.npr.org)

This national public radio station in the U.S. offers news and entertainment shows in English but does not have simplified English shows or lesson plans.

Voice of America (www.voanews.com)

Including simplified "special English" reports at http://www.voanews.com/specialenglish/

Yahooligans (www.yahooligans.com)

The search engine Yahoo's site for children and teens includes news, sports, entertainment, and games. This site also includes online tutors to help students with homework questions.

Miscellaneous sites

LD Pride (www.ldpride.net/learningstyles.MI.htm)

Information about multiple intelligences and learning styles, including free self-assessment tests. Note that although the site is aimed at people with learning disabilities, the information is useful for anyone interested in learning how the way we make use of different senses affects our learning.

Voice chat (www.mylanguageexchange.com/VoiceChat.asp)

This site enables students to practice speaking English with native speakers. The site provides free, helpful guidelines and tips on how to do a language exchange, as well as free lesson plans designed by an expert in language exchange learning.

Yahoo music (www.music.yahoo.com/) and MTV (www.mtv.com)

Both sites offer videos, songs, and news about music.

References

Day, R.R. and J. Bamford. 1998. *Extensive Reading in the Second Language Classroom.* Cambridge, UK: Cambridge University Press.

Gardner, Howard. 1999. *Intelligence Reframed: Multiple Intelligences for the 21st Century.* New York, NY: Basic Books.

Kinsella, K. 1995. Understanding and empowering diverse learners in the ESL classroom. In J. Reid (ed.) *Learning Styles in the ESL/EFL Classroom.* Boston: Newbury House/Heinle & Heinle.

Pugliese, C. 2005. Helping the students sing a better song: Multiple Intelligences Theory in the Classroom. Paper presented to a meeting of MICELT (Malaysia International Center for English Language Teaching), Damai Laut, Malaysia, April 26, 2005.

Richards, J. and R. Schmidt. 2003. *Longman Dictionary of Applied Linguistics.* London, UK: Longman.

Smith, Dorolyn. 2005. Worksheet for NPR News.

Stevick, Earl, quoted by Tim Bowen, "What is the silent way?" Download 6/20/05
http://www.onestopenglish.com/News/Magazine/Archive/silentway.htm

Appendix 1: Listening tasks

There's no such thing as a complete list of listening tasks. We're only limited by our imaginations. However, we seem to run into the same activities over and over again. Listed below are the listening tasks most often used in ESL or EFL classrooms all over the world. The purpose of this list is to stimulate your imagination.

Comprehension questions

Certainly the least creative type of task, it is also the most common. Most are literal comprehension questions, which actually don't have much to do with checking real understanding. At a minimum, the students should know the questions before they listen so they know their purpose for listening.

- Dictation—make the questions part of the task by dictating them to students before they listen to the text.
- Fill in the blank
- Multiple choice
- Open answer
- Predict (guess) answers, then listen.
- True/false

Various tasks

- Do something faster than the people on the tape do it (a math problem, spell a word, etc.).
- Finish the sentence based on what you heard.
- Identify a sequence of events or steps.
- Identify how many males and females are speaking.
- Identify how many speakers there are.
- Identify the context (time, place, etc.).
- Identify the correct paraphrase/summary. (This is a TOEFL favorite.)
- Identify the relationship between the speakers.
- Identify things talked about/done on a list.
- Infer an answer and then write two to three words that gave you the hints.
- Infer how strongly speakers feel about their opinions.
- Infer whether speakers agree or disagree with opinions and ideas.
- Infer the speaker's emotion or how strongly he or she feels.
- Infer the subject of a text.
- List things talked about or done.
- Listen and choose the correct response (another TOEFL favorite).
- Listen and write x number of pieces of information about each item.

- Listen to an explanation or interpretation of something (e.g., abstract or surreal art, a cartoon).
- Listen for the language function (e.g., *"You're late." Is that scolding? Informing?*). This is related to intonation.
- Paraphrase the text.
- Predict the response to a question.
- Predict the next line of a dialogue.
- Sort which information from a printed list is said by (or true about) which speaker.
- Write the reasons the speaker did something.

Picture this: art-based activities

These activities have students interacting with pictures. Some of them have students drawing pictures. When having students do this type of activity, we want students to focus on the meaning and not worry about drawing great pictures; therefore, we personally forbid erasers. It speeds things up.

- Draw a picture based on instructions or a description.
- Draw a picture based on your impression of a story (e.g., information given or inferred, or an emotional response).
- Find differences in text and pictures.
- Finish a partial picture.
- Identify pictures connected to short texts.
- Identify which picture the speakers are talking about.
- Label parts of a picture.
- Order the pictures in a text.

Maps, graphs, charts, etc.

- Fill in a chart/grid.
- Fill in a graph (e.g., change numbers into what they represent).
- Follow a route.
- Identify locations of objects or places.
- Write words/information on the appropriate place on a map.

Word/sentence level activities

- Correct grammatical errors, then listen to check.
- Count uses of a given word or sound.
- Count words in a sentence.
- Identify pauses and phrasing in sentences. (This works very well with songs.)
- Identify stress in a phrase or sentence. (Again, songs are great.)
- Identify the grammar form used.

- Note intonation by drawing arrows.
- Order words.

Imagination: it's all in your mind

- Guided Fantasy #1: Students listen to a story. Eyes closed—they imagine it (i.e., *Watch the movie in your mind*). At several points in the story, students make decisions. Later, they compare decisions.
- Guided Fantasy #2: Like Guided Fantasy #1, but with no particular decisions. Students just tell their stories and try to find things that are the same as or different from their classmates' stories.
- What's the Story?: Record a series of sounds. Students listen and imagine. Then they compare their ideas with their partner.
- Imaging Grammar #1: Listen to target sentences. Get a mental picture of the words. Follow spoken instructions (e.g., *In your mind, underline the verb.*).
- Imaging Grammar #2: Listen to the target structure. Get a mental picture that shows the meaning and mentally "write" the form next to the picture.
- Imaging Grammar #3: Listen to the target forms and mentally repeat them. (Students can experiment with voices—their own, a strong accent, etc.)
- Inner Voice: Listen to a conversation. After each exchange, guess what the speakers are thinking. (Note that this may need to be in the first language, at least at first.)
- Air Writing: While listening, "write" the sentences with a finger in the air or on a desk (a great activity for learners who are more tactile/kinesthetic).

Communicative dictation

Straight dictation in which students just write what they hear should be avoided, since it only involves bottom-up processing. However, dictation that makes students think can help them process top-down and bottom-up at the same time.

- Find differences between written and aural text.
- Jigsaw #1: Students hear different parts of a text. They talk to share their information.
- Jigsaw #2: Students hear two versions of the same text and find the differences.
- Jigsaw #3: Students find differences between aural and known text (e.g., *Little Blue Riding Hood*).
- Write dictated sentences, adding words at cued points.
- Evaluate a listening passage's ideas by writing sentences from the text under different headings (e.g., *yes/no, I agree/disagree*, etc.).
- Evaluate a passage's facts by preceding dictated sentences with *I think ...* or *I don't think ...* (e.g., *I don't think Japan has 300 islands.*) or by changing the verb

to the negative to show disagreement (e.g., Dictation sentence: *I have blond hair.* Students write: *I don't have blond hair.*).
- Write the opposite of what you hear (e.g., you say: *He's wearing black pants.* Students write: *She's wearing a white shirt.*).

What do you think? Opinions and affective responses
- Create an advertisement after listening to music from a TV commercial.
- Give opinions on four to six short bits of music, give a reason for the opinions, and state what type of person would like the music.
- Give an opinion on how to solve a problem in the listening passage.
- Give an opinion on whether or not a story is good and give a reason for the opinion. This can be done in the student's first language at lower levels.

The tape's talking to you.
- Answer opinion questions directed to the listener.
- Learn how to do something (meditation, massage, palm reading, etc.) and then do it.
- Physically follow instructions from a tape (e.g., *Raise your hand. Point to the window.*).
- Answer informational questions directed to the listener.

Appendix 2: Audio scripts

These correspond to the *Practical English Language Teaching: Listening* audio program. If possible, we suggest you actually listen to the audio program rather than just reading the scripts to more fully experience what students would be experiencing.

Track 1: Practical English Language Teaching: Listening, by Marc Helgesen and Steven Brown. Copyright 2006. McGraw-Hill ESL/ELT. No part of this publication may be reproduced or distributed in any form or by any means, or stored in a database or retrieval system, without the prior written consent of The McGraw-Hill Companies, Inc., including, but not limited to, in any network or other electronic storage or transmission, or broadcast for distance learning.

Track 2: Chapter 1, Example 2, Page 12
Active Listening 1: Listening for the Main Idea

Narrator: Part 1. Listen for the main idea. Listen. What is the most important idea? Check your answer.

(Phone rings, is picked up)
Paul: Hello?
Joan: Hi, Paul. This is Joan.
Paul: Oh, hi. How are you feeling? Are you still sick?
Joan: No, I feel better, thanks. I'm going to school tomorrow. What's the homework for English class?
Paul: The homework? Just a minute … OK, here it is. Read pages 23 and 24.
Joan: 23 and 24. OK. Thanks. See you tomorrow.
Paul: Bye.

Track 3: Chapter 1, Action Box, Page 14

This is in Korean. We are assuming most readers of this book do not speak Korean so we are using it to demonstrate how we can pick out pieces of information, even though the overall level of understanding is limited. The meaning of the Korean script is the same as that of the English script, Track 4.

Track 4: Chapter 1, Action Box, Page 14

Announcer: Here is the International Passenger Terminal 2, serving Korean Air, Asiana Airlines, Malaysia Airline System, Garuda Indonesia, Continental Airlines, Lauda Air, Lufthansa German Airlines, Swiss Air, Qantas Airways, and Alitalia. Next stop will be at the domestic passenger terminal. Thank you.

Track 5: Chapter 1, Example 3, Page 15
ICON 1: Have You Ever Been Abroad?

Interviewer: Welcome to Global Interviews. We have three guests, and we're talking about their travel experiences. Hi Marco, you're from Brazil, right?
Marco: Yes, that's right. I'm from Sao Paolo.
Interviewer: Have you ever been abroad?
Marco: Sure, I've been to Chile and to Canada. I spent a year in Ottawa. I was studying at the University.
Interviewer: Canada! I'll bet that was a change. Ottawa gets pretty cold in the winter.
Marco: Yeah, it was the first time I'd ever seen snow.
Interviewer: Did you go skiing?
Marco: Actually, I didn't have a chance to ski, but I did go skating. You know Ottawa has a lot of canals, so I skated to the university every day.

Interviewer: That's a different way to commute.

Marco: Yeah, it's better than driving. It beats the traffic in Sao Paulo.

Interviewer: Thanks, Marco. What about you, Minhee?

Minhee: I'm from Korea, from Seoul. Just like in San Paulo, the traffic there is terrible. I wish I could skate to work.

Interviewer: And do you ever travel?

Minhee: I've been to China and Australia, and I went to Japan last year.

Interviewer: Sounds like you've been to a lot of places in Asia. What was your most interesting travel experience?

Minhee: Interesting? I guess I would call it an interesting experience. It was when I took the wrong train. I was in Tokyo at Tokyo station and I wanted to take the bullet train, you know the Shinkansen to Atami, to visit a hot springs. So I got on the train and needed to get off at the fourth stop, which was Atami, but the train didn't stop. It just kept going very fast and the first stop was Nagoya.

Interviewer: Really? So what did you do?

Minhee: Well, there wasn't anything I could do, so I just relaxed. I got in to Nagoya and took another train back to Atami, but it took a long time.

Interviewer: Let me turn to our third guest, Ana. Where are you from?

Ana: I'm Mexican, but I live in Boston now.

Interviewer: Do you travel a lot?

Ana: Not very much, actually. But I have been to Morocco, and I have traveled around the US.

Interviewer: Morocco–that sounds interesting. How was it?

Ana: Great, I went to Marrakesh and Marabat.

Interviewer: What was your most interesting experience?

Ana: I can think of two. I really like the Souk, it's the outdoor market–they sell everything from jewelry to food. The other interesting experience was riding on a camel.

Interviewer: You rode on a camel? What was that like?

Ana: It was very uncomfortable. And my camel only wanted to lie down; it wouldn't stand up or walk.

Interviewer: Sounds like it was a short trip. Well, thanks to you all for these interesting experiences and for joining us on Global Interviews.

Track 6: Chapter 1, Example 4, Page 16 Good News, Bad News: Story 10

Narrator: Listen to the story. Then check the best summary.

A helicopter piloted by a woman lifted a prisoner from a rooftop of La Santé Prison in Paris on Monday and flew him out. The escaped prisoner was identified as Michel Vaujour, 34, who was found guilty of armed robbery last year. He was serving an 18-year sentence, and this was his fourth escape from prison.

Police said that a second prisoner decided at the last minute not to join Vaujour and surrendered.

According to police, the helicopter flew into the prison at about 10:45 A.M. and hovered over a prison building. Two people were aboard the aircraft, one armed with a machine gun. They dropped a line to Vaujour and then flew away.

A spokesperson for Air Continent, who owns the helicopter, said it had been rented by a woman about 30 years old.

Narrator: Before you listen again, try to number the pictures in the order the events happened. Then listen and check your work.

[story repeated]

Track 7: Chapter 2, Example 4, Page 42
Top-Up Listening 1: Let's Listen & Listening Clinic

Conversation 1:
Waitress: Good afternoon, sir.
Customer: Good afternoon.
Waitress: Are you ready to order, sir?
Customer: Uh … yes … er, a cup of coffee.
Waitress: Cream and sugar?
Customer: Just black, please.
Waitress: Anything else?
Customer: Yes, a piece of pie, please.
Waitress: What kind of pie would you like?
Customer: What do you have?
Waitress: We have apple, cherry, coconut cream, and lemon meringue.
Customer: Mmm, lemon meringue, please.
Waitress: 'Kay, so that's a cup of coffee and a piece of pie.
Customer: Yes, thanks.
Waitress: Coming right up.

Conversation 2
Waitress: Hi, what can I get you this evening?
Customer: Er, some clam chowder, please.
Waitress: A cup or a bowl?
Customer: A bowl, please.
Waitress: Very good, sir. Anything to drink?
Customer: Yes, uh, a Coke, please.
Waitress: Large or small?
Customer: Oh, just a small, please.

Waitress: Very good, sir. A bowl of chowder and a Coke.

The script for "Listening Clinic" appears on the student page reproduced on page 43.

Track 8: Chapter 2, Example 5, Page 44
Developing Tactics in Listening: Let's Listen

Narrator: People are talking about their vacations. Listen and number the topics 1 to 4 in the order they are mentioned.

Los Angeles is really beautiful. Everyone is so healthy and perfect-looking, but kind of unfriendly. This afternoon, I was parking my car at the beach when this man in a pickup truck started yelling at me. He said it was *his* parking space. At a public parking lot! We had to find another parking space, which wasn't easy, and it really scared my kids. When we finally got to the beach, it was just beautiful. We watched one of those great, slow California sunsets, then we had a delicious seafood dinner. After that, we drove back to our hotel and ordered dessert in our room—apple pie and vanilla ice cream! The hotel staff was helpful, and they were very nice to my kids. I really appreciated that.

Track 9: Chapter 2, Example 6, Page 46
Active Listening 1: This tastes great!

Narrator: Listen. People are eating diffferent foods. They don't say the names of the foods. What are they talking about? Number the pictures (1–6). There are two extra pictures.

1. Man: Do you want chocolate or vanilla?
Woman: Uh … chocolate, I guess.
Man: Here you go.
Woman: Thanks. Hmm … this tastes great. Nothing like it on a hot day.

2. (Sound of doorbell, followed by door being opened).
First Woman: Hi.
Man: Here it is. That's $12.50.
First Woman: Here you go. Keep the change.
Man: Thanks. (sound of door closing)
First Woman: It's here.
Second Woman: Great. You ordered a big one?
First Woman: Yeah. The fourteen-inch size.
Second Woman: What toppings?
First Woman: Let's see…there are mushrooms, onions, black olives, green peppers, and extra cheese.
Second Woman: Sounds great. I'll get some soda from the fridge.

3. First Man: Do you use cream or sugar?
Second Man: No, just black.
First Man: There's more when you finish. I made a whole pot.
Second Man: I'm not human without a cup in the morning.
First Man: I know what you mean.

Track 10: Chapter 2, Example 7, Page 47
Active Listening 1: Do you believe it?

3. 2003-year-old statue has face of rock star
Woman: Scientists in Greece found a statue that is over two thousand years old. The statue looks just like the famous rock-and-roll star Elvis Presley. How could the statue look like the American music star? The scientists say they don't know. Elvis's fans say it's proof he lived before.

4. Man loses one hundred pounds
Man: Roger Simms was overweight for years. His doctor told him to lose weight. If he didn't, he would get sick. Roger took the doctor's advice … too seriously, maybe. He lost one hundred pounds–that's nearly forty-five kilograms. How did he do it? By eating only watermelon. He ate watermelon for breakfast. Watermelon for lunch. And dinner? Watermelon. How does he feel now? Happy… and tired of eating watermelon.

Track 11: Chapter 2, Example 8, Page 48
English Firsthand 1: (music selection)

Track 12: Chapter 3, Example 1, Page 71
Sound Bytes 2: The Professor

Narrator: Part 2. What should you do during a job interview? Listen and check the sentences you hear.

The Professor: Greetings. Today I want to give you some tips on how to make a good impression at a job interview with an international company.
Ready? Now, let's think about what you should do before the interview–remember, preparation is very important. First, write down all the reasons you want the job, because the interviewer will probably ask you this. You should also write down other questions you think the interviewer will ask you about your work experience, your strong and weak points and any special skills you have. Of course, you should also think of good answers. Oh, one more thing: Think of at least one question for you to ask the interviewer about the job. This shows you are serious and have prepared well.

Track 13: Chapter 3, Example 2, Page 73
English Firsthand 2: Dear Editor

Dear Editor,
Discrimination is wrong. These days, everyone agrees that people who dislike other people because of their skin color or nationality are foolish racists. But what

about sexual discrimination and sexual harassment? On campus, it takes many forms. Some professors pay more attention to male students than to women. The men, they say, will become political and business leaders. Others pay attention to the women but for the wrong reasons. We don't want comments about our fashion and our bodies. We are in school to improve our minds. And, when we go to parties with male students, we want respect. No unwanted touching. Treat us like we are your equals. We are!
Sunny Wu

Track 14: Chapter 3, Example 3, Page 74
Listen In Book 3: Exercise 5

Narrator: Task 5. In spoken English, a /w/ sound is sometimes inserted between words in a process known as intrusion. Listen to the example. Example.
Woman: I never do/w/ any emailing. I never do/w/ any emailing.
Narrator: Look at these sentences and predict where you might hear a /w/ intrusion. Then listen and check. Listen again and practice with a partner. Can you think of any rules for when /w/ intrusion might take place?
Narrator: 1.
Man: I have no/w/online access from this computer.
Narrator: 2.
Woman: Helen isn't an Internet addict, but you/w/are!
Narrator: 3.
Man: Even though/w/I was really tired, I had to go/w/on.
Narrator: 4.
Woman: Go/w/under the bridge, then go through/w/another tunnel.
Narrator: 5.
Man: You/w/and I are going to/w/an event tonight.

Narrator: 6.
Woman: I have to do/w/another two/w/exercises before I can finish.

Track 15: Chapter 3, Example 4, Page 75
Active Listening 3: Your type of personality

Narrator: Listen. If the information on page 42 is true, what do you think these people's blood types are? What helped you guess? Write two or three things about each person.
Number 2. This is Jenny.

Jenny: I'm definitely a leader-type. I'm good at organizing things ... and people. That's one of the things I like about my job. I'm responsible for setting up projects. About the only thing I don't like is my boss. She's a nice person and all, but she always tells me exactly how to do everything. I don't like that at all. People work best when they have more freedom—to figure out the best way to do something by themselves. At least I work best that way.

Track 16: Chapter 3, Example 5, Page 76
Impact Listening 3: Real World Listening

Narrator: Unit 17 Self-Study. Listen to the conversation. Fill in the missing parts.
Whitney: Welcome to Life's Concerns. I'm your host, Whitney Opal. Today our program is about dealing with loss. One of the hardest things in life is losing a spouse after so many years together. Mr. Clayton Hayes is here today to share his story. Thank you for joining us, Mr. Hayes.
Clayton: Call me Clayton, please.
Whitney: Okay, Clayton. I'd like to ask you a few questions about how you're managing. Is that okay?
Clayton: Yes, that's fine. I can talk about it.
Whitney: All right. Well, your wife passed away two years ago—is that correct?

Clayton: Yep. Maggie was 79, just about to turn 80 when she passed away. I never really expected her to go. She was still too young.

Whitney: I'm sorry. Do you mind telling us how she died?

Clayton: Cancer. She had it for about a year, but it seemed longer than that to me. And she was in so much pain at the end. Oh.

Whitney: I'm, really sorry. That must have been very difficult for you.

Clayton: Yeah. At the end there, you could tell she just wanted it to be over. She tried to keep up a cheerful face for me, but you can't hide things from someone you've been married to for 56 years, you know.

Whitney: I'm sure that's true. You get to know someone pretty well in 56 years, don't you?

Clayton: Oh, you bet you do. You share so many years of your life with someone, and when they're gone, oh, there's a big hole that no one can fill up. You just feel lonely, very, very lonely.

Whitney: I imagine you have some wonderful memories, as well.

Clayton: Oh, yeah. We had a lot of good times, Maggie and me. Boy, the stories I could tell!

Whitney: Well, Clayton, you sure do have a lot of memories from your time with Maggie to celebrate!

Clayton: Yeah, I sure do.

Whitney: I think it's important to remember that when we lose someone close to us, we don't lose those memories. The person is still with us in that way.

Track 17: Chapter 3, Example 7, Page 79 *ICON 2:* That's really handy

Narrator: Page 63. Activity 2B. Second listening. Listen again and check the questions and comments you hear.

Clerk: Hi, welcome to Rocky's Emporium, home of a thousand electronic gifts. I'll be right with you.

Customer 3: Hi, I'm looking for this whatchamacallit I saw in your catalogue. I can't remember what it's called. You know, it helps you find your car keys when you lose them.

Clerk: Oh, the Key Finder. They're over there. I'll show you where they are.

Customer 3: Thanks.

Clerk: So, this is the Key Finder. When you lose your car keys, you push this button and it makes a noise ... like this.

Customer 3: That is so cool! You mean you just press this thing and it finds your keys? That is really handy. My Dad needs one of these. He's always losing his car keys and then he says I took them.

Clerk: It is a great gift. Can I get you anything else today?

Track 18: Chapter 3, Example 11, Page 84 *English Firsthand 2:* This is Meg.

Narrator: Number 3. This is Meg.

Interviewer: Meg, can you tell us about your future? Your goals?

Meg: Yes. I want to be happy.

Interviewer: You want to be happy?

Meg: Yeah, I just want to be happy.

Interviewer: And that's your goal?

Meg: Sure. I mean, most people talk about jobs and money and that kind of thing. But I don't think that makes anyone happy. I think I can be happy by helping people.

Interviewer: Yeah, maybe that's true, but, you know, what about making a living?

Meg: I'm not sure yet, but I think I want to be a teacher. You know, a helping kind of a job.

Interviewer: Well, are you doing anything now to help you prepare for that?

Meg: Yes, um, I'm a volunteer. On weekends there's a program where you read stories to little kids. I like that a lot.

Interviewer: Ah. You read to children?

Meg: Yea, um, it's fun. It makes me happy.

Interviewer: That's great.

Track 19: Chapter 5, Example 1, Page 132 Randall's ESL Cyber Listening Lab

Hotel Clerk: Hello. Sunnyside Inn. May I help you?

Man: Yes, I'd like to reserve a room for two on the 21st of March.

Hotel Clerk: Okay. Let me check our books here for a moment. The 21st of May, right?

Man: No. March, not May.

Hotel Clerk: Oh, sorry. Let me see here. Hmmm.

Man: Are you all booked that night?

Hotel Clerk: Well, we do have one suite available, complete with a kitchenette and a sauna bath. And the view of the city is great, too.

Man: How much is that?

Hotel Clerk: It's only $200 dollars, plus a 10% room tax.

Man: Oh, that's a little too expensive for me. Do you have a cheaper room available either on the 20th or the 22nd?

Hotel Clerk: Well, would you like a smoking or non-smoking room?

Man: Non-smoking, please.

Hotel Clerk: Okay, we have a few rooms available on the 20th; we're full on the 22nd, unless you want a smoking room.

Man: Well, how much is the non-smoking room on the 20th?

Hotel Clerk: $80 dollars, plus the 10% room tax.

Man: Okay, that'll be fine.

Hotel Clerk: All right. Could I have your name, please?

Man: Yes. Bob Maexner.

Hotel Clerk: How do you spell your last name, Mr. Maexner?

Man: M-A-E-X-N-E-R.

Hotel Clerk: Okay, Mr. Maexner, we look forward to seeing you on March 20th.

Man: Okay. Goodbye.

Glossary

accuracy – work in which the learner is focused on correctness, especially grammatical correctness

acquisition – the unconscious ability to understand and use language

active skill – a skill that requires learners to engage with the input consciously– usually by making an observable response

ALM (Audio-Lingual Method) – a drill-based method based on behavioristic psychology and structural linguistics

assessment – collecting information and making judgments on a learner's knowledge

authentic texts – spoken and written language which is created for the purpose of genuine communication rather than being especially created for the purposes of language learning and teaching

autonomy – the capacity to control one's own learning

back channel – to use words or utterances that show the speaker the listener is attending to what is being said

bottom-up processing – using component parts–words, grammar, and the like– to process meaning

clarifying – a strategy in which the learner actively questions the speaker to make sure understanding is taking place

cloze activity – a listening or reading exercise in which words have been deleted from a text and replaced by a blank

Communicative Language Teaching – a language teaching method based on interaction in the target language

communicative test – a test that simulates what learners are required to do in the real world

connotation – the non-dictionary meaning of a word

criterion-referenced testing – the interpretation of assessment results in relation to an external standard

critical listening – listening with the goal of critiquing or understanding more deeply the message of the text

cultural literacy – fluency in the idioms, allusions, and informal content of language that stems from historic or popular culture

dictation – an exercise in which someone reads or speaks and others write down what was said

direct testing – assessment of a skill itself, e.g., a test of listening in which the learner has to discriminate between two sounds that have been taught

direction of processing – how people try to make sense of what they hear, top-down, bottom-up, or interactively

discourse – language at a level beyond the sentence

discourse markers – phrases in speech that help to organize a text or indicate a speaker is transitioning to the next logical piece of information

discrete test items – items which measure small pieces of language such as phonemes or pieces of grammar

elaborated text – real-world text that has been adapted for use in the classroom

English as a Foreign Language (EFL) – a situation in which English is not the language of communication in the larger society (e.g., learning English in China or Japan)

English as a Second Language (ESL) – a situation in which English is the language of communication in the larger society (e.g., learning English in the United States or Australia)

evaluation – a strategy in which the learner looks back on the course or lesson and reflects on the amount and process of learning

extensive listening – listening to long stretches of language such as movies and TV shows

false beginner – a learner who has studied a language for several years and has knowledge of its vocabulary and structures, but who cannot use the language fluently

false start – a beginning made to an utterance that is stopped for some reason

fluency – work in which the learner is focused exclusively or primarily on meaning; may or may not include native-like speed, phrasing, etc. since the person is in the process of learning

Focus on Form (FonF) – an approach to teaching in which the learner's attention is drawn to the structure of the language

functional language – language analyzed by its use rather than its grammar

functional phrases – small pieces of language that are used to accomplish something in that language (e.g., functional phrases for apologies in English include *Excuse me* and *I'm sorry*)

gist listening – listening to understand the main ideas

global listening – see **listening for gist**

graphic organizer – a pictorial representation of the ideas of a text, sometimes given to learners before listening and sometimes a way of representing what was heard

idea units – groups of words or phrases which may not be complete sentences, but which convey a definite meaning

indirect testing – assessment on one aspect of language that is used to assess another aspect (e.g., using dictation of a text to assess grammatical knowledge)

inference – a guess or conclusion made from the context surrounding a text when the meaning is not stated directly

inferencing – to decide on an answer, idea, or judgement, based on information that is not directly stated. The term is often used in teaching, meaning essentially the same thing as inferring or making inferences

information transfer questions – questions which require learners to change the way something is represented (e.g., by choosing a picture that shows what was heard)

input – spoken or written language that is made available to learners as a basis for learning

intake – input which the learner actually pays attention to and uses for acquisition

Intensive English Programs (IEPs) – usually at the college or university level, classes for learners of English that focus on distinct skills—reading, writing, listening, and speaking—at the beginning, intermediate, and advanced levels

interactive processing – the use of both top-down and bottom-up processing at the same time

jigsaw listening – a listening activity in which different learners hear different pieces of information and must combine their knowledge to understand the whole text

learning strategies – characteristics and techniques students use to enable them to become proficient and efficient learners

lingua franca – a common language in a country that has many languages, or a language used across countries

listening center – a place where learners can go to listen independently

listening for gist – listening to understand the main idea, also **global listening**

listening for specific information – listening to understand details

literal processing – listening to understand exactly what was said

making inferences – listening and then guessing the meaning in context

metacognitive strategies – learning strategies which require students to think about their learning, organize it, and reflect on it

mind map – a kind of graphic organizer, often used to take notes while listening

monitoring – the strategy learners use to pay attention to their learning process, their feelings about learning, and their plans for future learning

multiple intelligences (MI) – the various ways people relate to the world

non-reciprocal listening – listening in which the listener does not respond to the speaker

normative testing – the interpretation of assessment results in terms of the performance of the group that was tested

open-ended tasks – tasks that don't require a specific response

passive skill – a skill that does not require the learner to be consciously engaged

pedagogical tasks – tasks that occur in the classroom

performance-based testing – direct assessment of the learner's skills

personalize – adapt the activity to make it relevant to the learners' lives, to allow them to relate the text to themselves

phonemes – meaning-bearing units of sound in a particular language

portfolio – a form of assessment in which learners keep and give to the teacher examples of their work in the course in an organized fashion

practicality – the extent to which the demands of giving an assessment are reasonable

predicting – the strategy learners use to guess what will come next in a text or lesson

presentation→practice→production (PPP) – a common model for language teaching in which learners are first presented with the language and given opportunities to practice before they are expected to produce

productive skill – a skill that requires a learner to be engaged and make a response

prosody – sound characteristics such as stress, intonation, loudness, pitch, and duration of syllables

receptive skill – a skill that does not require a learner to make a response (e.g., When we say listening is a receptive skill, we imply that learners do need to think about the input consciously, but they may not need to make an observable response.)

reciprocal listening – listening in which the listener makes a response to the speaker

redundancy – saying the same thing again, either simply repeating or using different words

reliability – the extent to which an assessment consistently measures language behavior

responding – the strategy learners use to get more input

responsive listening – exercises that ask the learner to listen to a question and choose from several answers, or listen to a conversation and answer questions about it

role play – a speaking activity in which learners take on the identities of other people and behave as they would behave

schema – the interrelated knowledge patterns in our mind, usually based on prior knowledge or experience

schemata – plural of schema

self-assessment – learners collecting information and making judgments on their own knowledge

target tasks – tasks that learners will do with their language once they leave class

task – an activity which learners carry out using their available language resources and leading to a real outcome

task awareness – the knowledge learners have of what a task demands of them

Task-based Learning (TBL) – an approach based on the use of communicative and interactive tasks as the central units for the planning and delivery of instruction

text – a stretch of language, written or spoken

top-down processing – using background knowledge to process meaning

Total Physical Response (TPR) – a language learning activity in which learners listen and do the action that the teacher says

true beginner – a learner who starts language study with no background in the language

validity – the extent to which an assessment is appropriate for its intended purposes

washback – the effect that an assessment has on what is taught and how it is taught

Index

Credits

p. 7 from *The Language Teaching Matrix.* by Jack C. Richards, 1990. Reprinted by permission of Cambridge University Press. **p.** 10 from *Listen in 3, 2nd edition* by David Nunan, 2003. Reprinted by permission of Heinle, a division of Thomson Learning, Reprinted by permission of the McGraw-Hill companies for class use. All rights reserved. Aside from this specific exception, no part of this book may be reproduced, stored in a retrieval system, or transcribed in any form of by any means—electronic, mechanical, photocopying, recording or otherwise—without permission in writing from the Thomson Learning Global Rights Group. **p.** 12 from *Active Listening 3: Expanding Understanding through Content* by Marc Helgesen, Steven Brown, and D. Smith, 1996. Reprinted with the permission of Cambridge University Press. **p.** 15 from *Icon 1* by Donald Freeman, Kathleen Graves, and Linda Lee, 2005. Reprinted by permission of The McGraw-Hill Companies, Inc. **p.** 16 from *Good News, Bad News* by Roger Barnard, 1998. **p.** 30 Questionnaire from "Good Learning Task" from *Task-Based Language Teaching* by David Nunan, 2004. Reprinted with the permission of Cambridge University Press. **p.** 38 from *Icon Intro* by Donald Freeman, Kathleen Graves, and Linda Lee, 2005. Reprinted by permission of The McGraw-Hill Companies, Inc. **p.** 39 *Listen in 1* (with Audio CD) 2nd edition by David Nunan, 2003. Reprinted by permission of Heinle, a division of Thomson Learning, Reprinted by permission of the McGraw-Hill companies for class use. All rights reserved. Aside from this specific exception, no part of this book may be reproduced, stored in a retrieval system, or transcribed in any form of by any means—electronic, mechanical, photocopying, recording or otherwise—without permission in writing from the Thomson Learning Global Rights Group. **p.** 40 from *English Firsthand 1* by Marc Helgesen, Steven Brown, and Tom Mandeville, 2004. **p.** 43 from *Top-Up Listening 1* by ABAX Publishing, (Cleary, Holden, and Cooney, Series Ed. M. Jamall, 2003, pp. 22–23). Reprinted with permission ABAX Ltd. **p.** 44 from *Developing Tactics for Listening* by Jack C. Richards Reprinted with the permission of Cambridge University Press. 2003. **pp.** 46 & 47 from *Active Listening 1: Introducing Skills for Understanding* by Marc Helgesen, Steven Brown, 1996. Reprinted with the permission of Cambridge University Press. **p.** 48 from *English Firsthand 1* by Marc Helgesen, Steven Brown, and Tom Mandeville, 2004. **p.** 51 from *English Firsthand 1 Teachers Manual* by Marc Helgesen, Steven. Brown and Tom Mandeville, 2004. **p.** 71 from *Sound Bytes 2* by S. Gershon and C. Mares, 2000. **p.** 73 from *English Firsthand 2* by Marc Helgesen, Steven Brown and Tom Mandeville, 2004. **p.** 74 from *Listen in 3* (with Audio CD) 2nd edition by David Nunan, 2003 Reprinted by permission of Heinle, a division of Thomson Learning, Reprinted by permission of the McGraw-Hill companies for class use. All rights reserved. Aside from this specific exception, no part of this book may be reproduced, stored in a retrieval system, or transcribed in any form of by any means—electronic, mechanical, photocopying, recording or otherwise—without permission in writing from the Thomson Learning Global Rights Group. **p.** 75 from *Active Listening 3: Expanding Understanding through Content* by Marc Helgesen, Steven Brown, and D. Smith, 1996. Reprinted with the permission of Cambridge University Press. **p.** 76 *Impact Listening 3* by Kenton Harsch and Kate Wolfe-Quintero, 2001. **p.** 78 from *English Firsthand 2 Teachers Edition Manual* by Marc Helgesen, Steven Brown, and Tom Mandeville, 2004. **p.** 79 from *Icon 2* by Donald Freeman, Kathleen Graves, and Linda Lee, 2005. Reprinted by permission of The McGraw-Hill Companies, Inc. **p.** 80 from "Beating Around the Bush" by Maley from *Top Class Activities 2* edited by Peter Watcyn-Jones, 2000. **p.** 81 From *Active Listening 3: Expanding Understanding through Content* by Marc Helgesen, Steven Brown, and D. Smith, 1996. Reprinted with the permission of Cambridge University Press. **p.** 82 *Language Hungry* by Tim Murphey, 1998. **p.** 84 from *English Firsthand 2 Teachers Edition Manual* by Marc Helgesen, Steven Brown, and Tom Mandeville, 2004. **p.** 91 from *Tapestry Listening & Speaking 3*, 2nd *edition* by Karen Carlisi and Susana Christie Carlisi, 2000 Reprinted by permission of Heinle, a division of Thomson Learning, Reprinted by permission of the McGraw-Hill companies for class use. All rights reserved. Aside from this specific exception, no part of this book may be reproduced, stored in a retrieval system, or transcribed in any form of by any means—electronic, mechanical, photocopying, recording or otherwise—without permission in writing from the Thomson Learning Global Rights Group. **p.** 92 from "Learner Strategy Training in the Classroom: An Action Research Study", *TESOL Journal*, 6, 96 by David Nunan, 1996. Reprinted by permission of TESOL. **p.** 93 From *Active Listening 3: Expanding Understanding through Content* by Marc Helgesen, Steven Brown, and D. Smith, 1996. Reprinted with the permission of Cambridge University Press. **p.** 99 from *Quest 3 Listening and Speaking in the Academic World* by Pamela Hartmann and Laurie Blass, 2000. Reprinted by permission of The McGraw-Hill Companies, Inc. **p.** 101 from *Encarta World English Dictionary* by Anne H. Soukhanov, 1999. **pp.** 104 & 105 from *Talk it Over!*. By Joann Kozyrev, 2002. Reprinted with permission by Houghton Mifflin Company. **p.** 107 from *English Firsthand 2* by Marc Helgesen, Steven Brown and Tom Mandeville, 2004. **p.** 108 from *On the Air: Listening to Radio Talk* by C. Sadow and E. Sather, 1998. Reprinted with the permission of Cambridge University Press. **p.** 110 from *The Context of Language Teaching* by Jack C. Richards, 1985. **pp.** 110-113 from *Quest 3 Listening and Speaking in the Academic World* by Pamela Hartmann and Laurie Blass, 2000. Reprinted by permission of The McGraw-Hill Companies, Inc. **p.** 114 from *Listening Extra* by Miles Craven, 2004. Reprinted with the permission of Cambridge University Press. **p.** 115 From *Impact Listening 3* by Kenton Harsch and Kate Wolfe-Quintero, 2001. **p.** 116 from *Icon 3* by Donald Freeman, Kathleen Graves, and Linda Lee, 2005.

Practical English Language Teaching: Listening
Audio CD Tracking Information